KETCHUP VOCA

LEVEL 2 ②

i-Scream edu

영어 공부의 핵심은 단어입니다.

케찹보카로
영어 단어 실력을 키우고,
상위 1% 어휘력을
따라잡아 보세요!

케찹보카 친구들

Dennis	엉뚱하고 낙천적인 성격의 자유로운 영혼! 예측 불가에, 공부에도 관심이 없지만, 운이 좋아 뭘 해도 잘 풀린대요.	
Rod	인내심이 크고 생각도 깊은, 다정다감 엄친아! 개구쟁이 쌍둥이 누나, 애완묘 루나가 있어 혼자 있는 것보단 함께 하는 것을 좋아해요.	
Kiara	노래를 좋아하는 사교성의 아이콘! 솔직하고 모든 일에 적극적이지만, 금방 사랑에 빠지는 짝사랑 전문가래요.	
Sally	논리적이고 긍정적인 모범생! 친구들과 장난도 많이 치지만, 호기심이 많아 관심 분야에 다양한 지식을 갖고 있어요.	
Mong	친구들이 궁금한 것이 있을 때 나타나는 해결사! 너무 아는 것이 많아서 어느 별에서 왔는지 궁금하기도 해요.	

만화 스토리

친구들의 좌충우돌 일상이 그려진
재미있는 만화를 보며
단어 뜻을 배우고,
문장에 어떻게 활용되는지
알아볼 수 있어요!

어휘력이란?
문맥 속에서 의미를 알고
표현적으로 사용할 수 있는 능력을 뜻합니다.

Know Exercise Think Check Habit

KETCH UP

망각 제로 단어 기억하기 습관으로
기억 장기화

게임으로 즐겁게 리뷰하고 테스트로 더블 체크

만화 스토리 〉 단어 〉 문장 순으로
단어 의미를 이해하며 모국어처럼 습득

이미지 연상 쓰기 연습으로 실제 단어 활용, 적용

주제별로 초등 필수&고난도 단어 학습하며
상위 1% 단어 마스터

KETCHUP
makes you Catch up.

Let's catch up with KETCHUP VOCA!

How to Use

체계적인 4 Steps 시스템으로 학습 완성!

	Step 1	Step 2	Step 3	Step 4
Day 1~4	●	●	●	
Day 5	●	●	●	●

Step 1

Warm up 망각 제로&스토리 단어 이해로 학습 준비하기

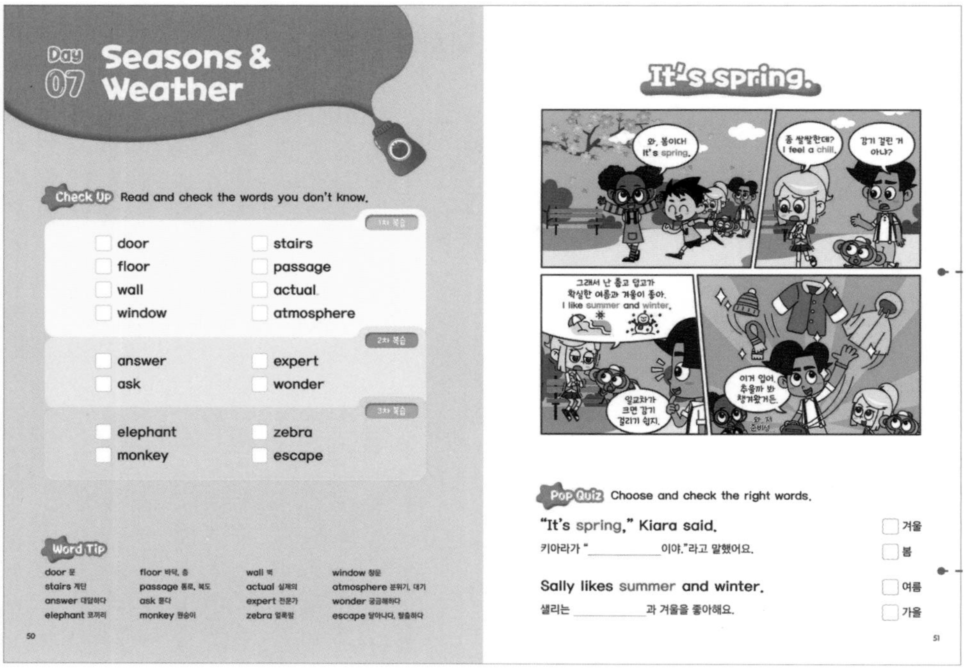
Day 07 Seasons & Weather

Check Up Read and check the words you don't know.

1차 복습
□ door □ stairs
□ floor □ passage
□ wall □ actual
□ window □ atmosphere

2차 복습
□ answer □ expert
□ ask □ wonder

3차 복습
□ elephant □ zebra
□ monkey □ escape

Word Tip
door 문 / floor 바닥, 층 / wall 벽 / window 창문
stairs 계단 / passage 통로, 복도 / actual 실제의 / atmosphere 분위기, 대기
answer 대답하다 / ask 묻다 / expert 전문가 / wonder 궁금해하다
elephant 코끼리 / monkey 원숭이 / zebra 얼룩말 / escape 달아나다, 탈출하다

50

It's spring.

Pop Quiz Choose and check the right words.

"It's spring," Kiara said. □ 겨울
키아라가 "________ 이야."라고 말했어요. □ 봄

Sally likes summer and winter. □ 여름
샐리는 ________ 과 겨울을 좋아해요. □ 가을

51

만화를 보며
단어 뜻 이해하기

문장에 적용하여
단어 뜻 찾기

※ 망각 제로는 p10에서 확인하세요!

Step 2

Catch up 듣고, 말하고, 읽고, 쓰며, 상위 1% 단어 따라잡기

QR 찍어 단어 듣고 따라 말하기 ▶ 케찹병을 색칠하며 3번 반복하기

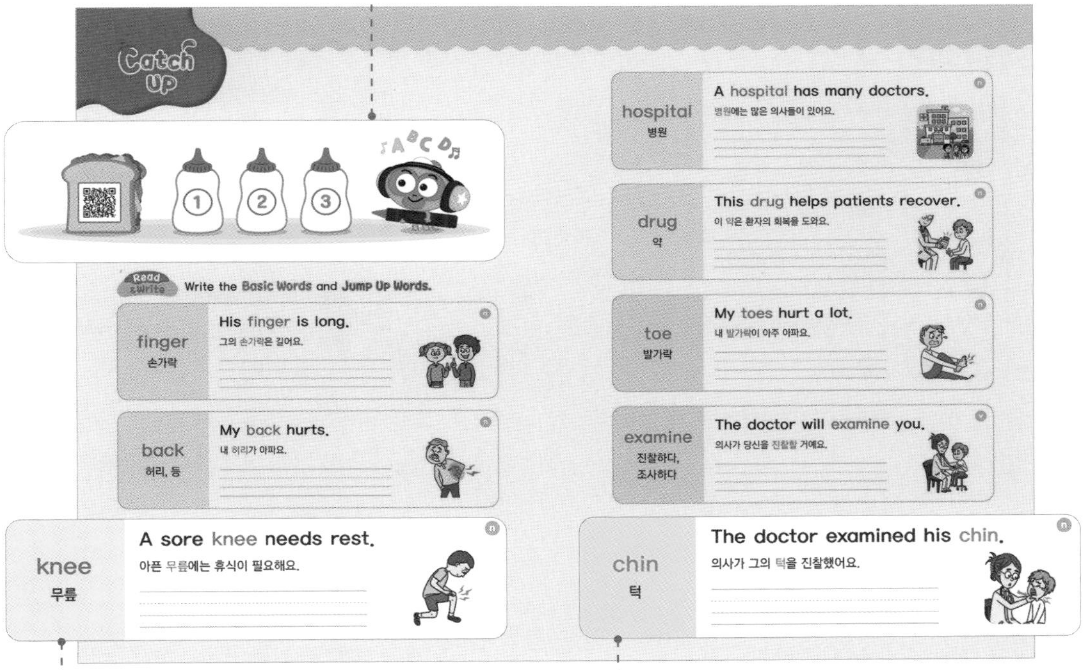

Basic Words 초등 필수 단어

Jump Up Words 고난도 단어

품사 기호

v	verb (동사)	adv	adverb (부사)	conj	conjunction (접속사)
n	noun (명사)	prep	preposition (전치사)	pron	pronoun (대명사)
a	adjective (형용사)	det	determiner (한정사)	num	numeral (수사)

케찹보카와 함께
상위 1% CATCH UP!

Step 3

Skill up 두뇌 자극 이미지 연상 학습으로 실력 강화하기

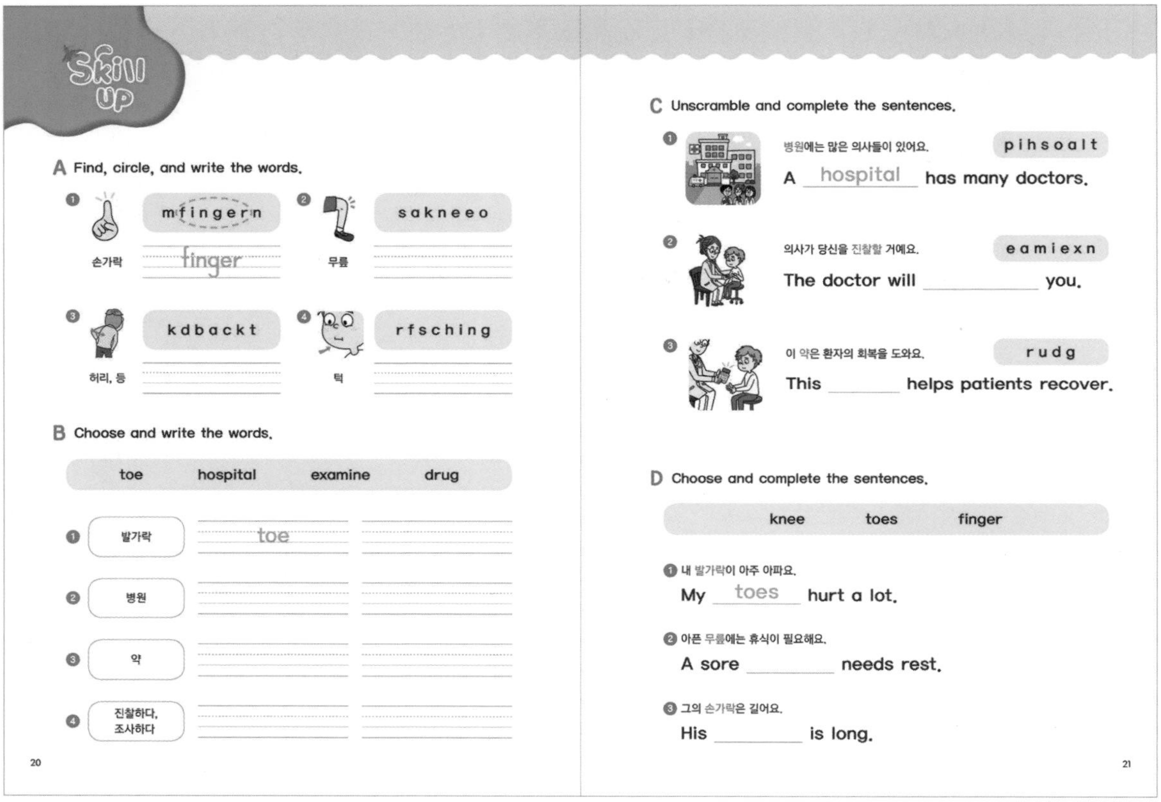

Skill UP

A Find, circle, and write the words.

❶ mfingern — 손가락 — finger
❷ sakneeo — 무릎
❸ kdbackt — 허리, 등
❹ rfsching — 턱

B Choose and write the words.

toe hospital examine drug

❶ 발가락 — toe
❷ 병원
❸ 약
❹ 진찰하다, 조사하다

20

C Unscramble and complete the sentences.

❶ 병원에는 많은 의사들이 있어요. pihsoalt
A hospital has many doctors.

❷ 의사가 당신을 진찰할 거예요. eamiexn
The doctor will ________ you.

❸ 이 약은 환자의 회복을 도와요. rudg
This ________ helps patients recover.

D Choose and complete the sentences.

knee toes finger

❶ 내 발가락이 아주 아파요.
My toes hurt a lot.

❷ 아픈 무릎에는 휴식이 필요해요.
A sore ________ needs rest.

❸ 그의 손가락은 길어요.
His ________ is long.

21

유형 1	유형 2	유형 3	유형 4
이미지 연상을 통해 단어 완성하기	우리말에 맞춰 스펠링 배열하여 단어 쓰기	이미지와 문장을 연결하여 단어 뜻 이해하기	배운 단어 적용하여 문장 완성하여 쓰기

Step 4

Wrap up 게임과 최종 평가를 통해 단어 학습 마무리하기

쉬어가기

다양한 유형의 재미있는 게임하며 단어 복습하기!

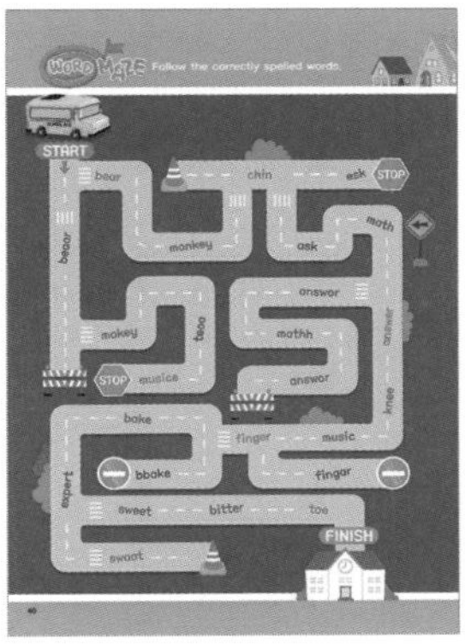

Word Maze
알맞은 스펠링으로 이뤄진 단어를 따라가 미로 찾기

Word Puzzle
주어진 문장에 알맞은 단어를 쓰며 퍼즐 완성하기

Word Search 1
힌트를 보고 알맞은 그림을 찾아 쓰기 연습하기

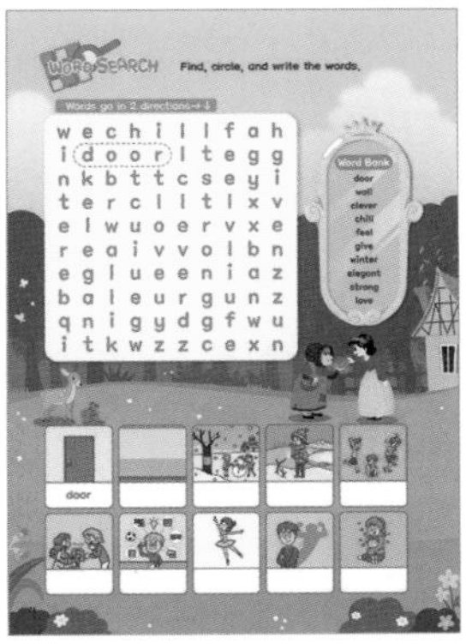

Word Search 2
다양한 알파벳 속 배운 단어를 찾아 쓰기 연습하기

복습&테스트

지금까지 배운 단어 정리하고, 테스트로 최종 점검!
뜯어서 쓰는 나만의 단어장까지!

Study Planner & Contents

Part I

Day 01 Performance

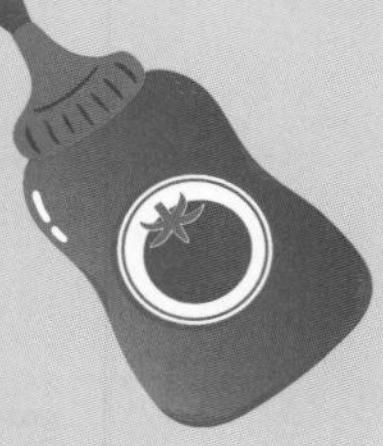

망각 제로란?

망각 제로는
학습 주기를 활용해서 복습하는 거야.

지난번에 공부했던 단어 중에
아는 것과 모르는 것을 확인해 볼 수 있겠네!

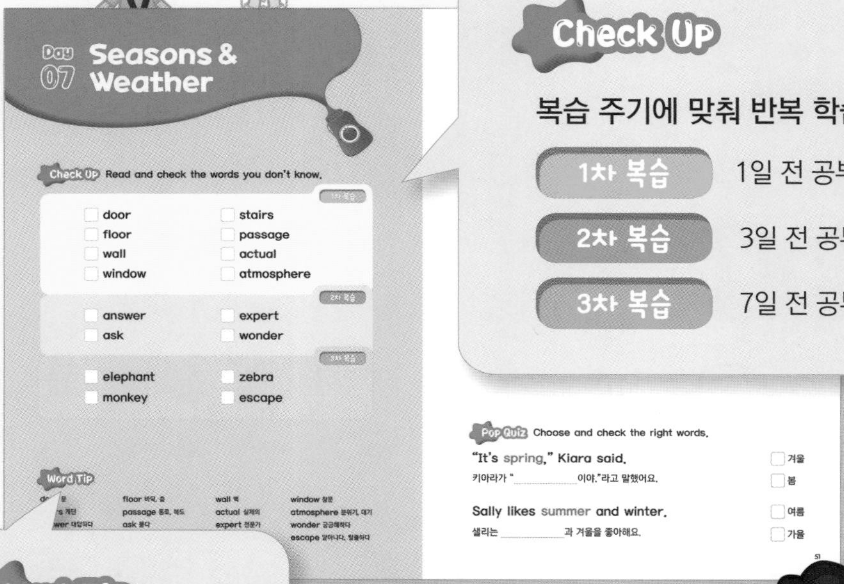

Day 07 Seasons & Weather

Check Up Read and check the words you don't know.

1차 복습
- door
- floor
- wall
- window
- stairs
- passage
- actual
- atmosphere

2차 복습
- answer
- ask
- expert
- wonder

3차 복습
- elephant
- monkey
- zebra
- escape

Word Tip

Pop Quiz Choose and check the right words.

"It's spring," Kiara said.
키아라가 "_______이야."라고 말했어요.
- 겨울
- 봄

Sally likes summer and winter.
샐리는 _______과 겨울을 좋아해요.
- 여름
- 가을

Check Up

복습 주기에 맞춰 반복 학습하기

1차 복습	1일 전 공부한 단어
2차 복습	3일 전 공부한 단어
3차 복습	7일 전 공부한 단어

Word Tip

정확한 단어 뜻 확인하기

"우리 같이
망각 제로 학습해 보자"

※ 망각 제로는 [DAY 02]부터 시작합니다.

We formed a band.

Pop Quiz Choose and check the right words.

There are many things in the garage.

차고에는 많은 ____________들이 있어요.

They formed a band.

아이들은 ____________를 만들었어요.

- [ ] 목표
- [x] 물건
- [ ] 밴드
- [ ] 조깅

Catch Up

Listen & Say Listen, say, and color.

Read & Write Write the **Basic Words** and **Jump Up Words.**

part
부분, 일부

n

I missed the first part of the performance.
나는 공연의 첫 부분을 놓쳤어요.

part

example
예

n

He gave me a good example.
그는 나에게 좋은 예시를 보여주었어요.

thing
것, 물건

n

There are lots of things to do.
할 것이 많아요.

band
밴드, 그룹

(n)

The band played well.

그 밴드는 연주를 잘했어요.

end
끝나다, 끝

(v) (n)

The show ended.

공연이 끝났어요.

aim
목표, 목표하다

(n) (v)

The guitarist's aim was to impress.

그 기타리스트의 목표는 감동을 주는 것이었어요.

jog
조깅, 조깅하다

(n) (v)

He took a quick jog.

그는 짧게 조깅했어요.

expect
기대하다,
예상하다

(v)

You can expect to enjoy the festival.

당신은 축제를 즐길 것이라고 기대할 수 있어요.

Skill UP

A Choose and write the words.

part end jog

1. 

jog

조깅, 조깅하다

2. 

부분, 일부

3. 

끝나다, 끝

B Choose and write the words.

expect aim example thing

1. 기대하다, 예상하다 — expect
2. 것, 물건
3. 목표, 목표하다
4. 예

C Unscramble and complete the sentences.

1 

그 밴드는 연주를 잘했어요.

d n b a

The band played well.

2 

그 기타리스트의 목표는 감동을 주는 것이었어요.

m i a

The guitarist's ________ was to impress.

3 

당신은 축제를 즐길 것이라고 기대할 수 있어요.

p x e t c e

You can ________ to enjoy the festival.

D Choose and complete the sentences.

example part jog

1 그는 짧게 조깅했어요.

He took a quick jog.

2 나는 공연의 첫 부분을 놓쳤어요.

I missed the first ________ of the performance.

3 그는 나에게 좋은 예시를 보여주었어요.

He gave me a good ________.

Day 02

Health

Check Up Read and check the words you don't know.

1차 복습

- [ ] part
- [ ] example
- [ ] thing
- [ ] band
- [ ] end
- [ ] aim
- [ ] jog
- [ ] expect

※망각 제로! 1일 전 학습한 단어를 복습해요.

Word Tip

part 부분, 일부	**example** 예	**thing** 것, 물건	**band** 밴드, 그룹
end 끝나다, 끝	**aim** 목표, 목표하다	**jog** 조깅, 조깅하다	**expect** 기대하다, 예상하다

Be careful not to catch a cold.

Pop Quiz Choose and check the right words.

Sally caught a cold.

샐리는 ____________에 걸렸어요.

☐ 감기
☐ 열

Sally has a fever and a headache.

샐리는 열이 나고 ____________이 있어요.

☐ 두통
☐ 건강

Catch Up

Listen & Say Listen, say, and color.

Read & Write Write the **Basic Words** and **Jump Up Words.**

cold
감기

n

I caught a cold.
나는 감기에 걸렸어요.

fever
열

n

He has a fever.
그는 열이 나요.

health
건강

n

We should exercise for our health.
우리는 건강을 위해 운동을 해야 해요.

fine

괜찮은, 좋은

a

My leg is fine.

내 다리는 괜찮아요.

headache

두통

n

I have a headache.

나는 두통이 있어요.

faint

어지러운, 희미한, 기절하다

a v

I suddenly felt faint.

나는 갑자기 어지러움을 느꼈어요.

revive

회복하다, 활기를 되찾다

v

A hot shower can help revive you.

뜨거운 샤워는 당신이 회복하는 데 도움을 줄 수 있어요.

decay

썩다, 부패하다

v

Sweets make your teeth decay.

단것은 당신의 이를 썩게 해요.

Skill UP

A Find, circle, and write the words.

1 감기 — c o l d e s t d — cold

2 어지러운, 희미한, 기절하다 — g q f a i n t y

3 열 — h f e v e r g y

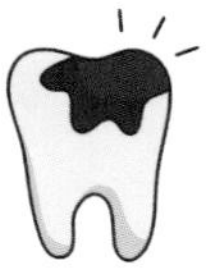

4 썩다, 부패하다 — s d e c a y l k

B Cross out, unscramble, and write the words.

1 괜찮은, 좋은 — i x n e f — fine

2 건강 — a g h l h t e

3 두통 — a h d e h c r a e

4 회복하다, 활기를 되찾다 — e u v i e v r

C Connect and fill in the blanks.

1 

2 

3 

We should exercise for our health.

우리는 ____________ 을 위해 운동을 해야 해요.

I have a headache.

나는 ____두통____ 이 있어요.

My leg is fine.

내 다리는 ____________ 요.

D Rearrange and write the sentences.

1 나는 감기에 걸렸어요.

I | a cold | caught | .

I caught a cold.

2 단것은 당신의 이를 썩게 해요.

make | decay | Sweets | your | teeth | .

Day 03 Communication

Check Up Read and check the words you don't know.

1차 복습

- [ ] cold
- [ ] fever
- [ ] fine
- [ ] revive
- [ ] headache
- [ ] faint
- [ ] health
- [ ] decay

※**망각 제로!** 1일 전 학습한 단어를 복습해요.

Word Tip

cold 감기 **fever** 열 **fine** 괜찮은, 좋은 **revive** 회복하다, 활기를 되찾다
headache 두통 **faint** 어지러운, 희미한, 기절하다 **health** 건강 **decay** 썩다, 부패하다

I'm sorry.

Pop Quiz Choose and check the right words.

Rod is mowing the lawn.

로드는 ____________를 깎고 있어요.

☐ 편지

☐ 잔디

Dennis said, "I'm sorry."

데니스는 ____________다고 말했어요.

☐ 적절한

☐ 미안한

Catch UP

Listen & Say Listen, say, and color.

Read & Write Write the **Basic Words** and **Jump Up Words.**

thank
감사하다,
고마워하다

v

I thank my teacher.

나는 우리 선생님께 감사드려요.

sorry
미안한,
안쓰러운

a

I am so sorry.

정말 미안해요.

again
다시,
한 번 더

adv

Can we play that game again?

그 게임을 다시 할 수 있을까요?

guide
안내하다,
이끌다

v

Can you **guide** me?
나를 안내해 줄 수 있나요?

letter
편지

n

I wrote a **letter** to my grandma.
나는 할머니께 편지를 썼어요.

proper
적절한,
올바른

a

It's important to use **proper** manners.
적절한 예의범절을 사용하는 것이 중요해요.

express
표현하다,
나타내다

v

I like to **express** my feelings.
나는 내 감정을 표현하는 것을 좋아해요.

lawn
잔디

n

Let's play catch on the **lawn**.
잔디 위에서 캐치볼을 하자.

Skill UP

A Choose and write the words.

lawn　　sorry　　guide

1 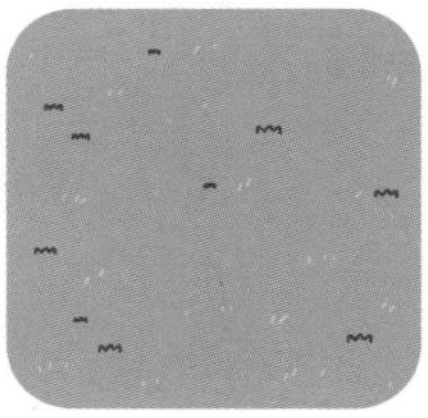

잔디

2 

안내하다, 이끌다

3 

미안한, 안쓰러운

B Choose and write the words.

express　　thank　　proper　　again

1 감사하다, 고마워하다

2 적절한, 올바른

3 다시, 한 번 더

4 표현하다, 나타내다

C Unscramble and complete the sentences.

1 

나는 우리 선생님께 감사드려요.

h a n t k

I ________ my teacher.

2 

나는 할머니께 편지를 썼어요.

t l e t r e

I wrote a ________ to my grandma.

3 

적절한 예의범절을 사용하는 것이 중요해요.

p o p r r e

It's important to use ________ manners.

D Choose and complete the sentences.

lawn guide express

1 나를 안내해 줄 수 있나요?

Can you ________ me?

2 잔디 위에서 캐치볼을 하자.

Let's play catch on the ________.

3 나는 내 감정을 표현하는 것을 좋아해요.

I like to ________ my feelings.

Day 04

Education

Check Up Read and check the words you don't know.

1차 복습

- [ ] thank
- [ ] sorry
- [ ] again
- [ ] guide
- [ ] letter
- [ ] proper
- [ ] express
- [ ] lawn

2차 복습

- [ ] part
- [ ] example
- [ ] jog
- [ ] expect

※망각 제로! 1일 전 3일 전 학습한 단어를 복습해요.

Word Tip

thank 감사하다, 고마워하다
sorry 미안한, 안쓰러운
again 다시, 한 번 더
guide 안내하다, 이끌다
letter 편지
proper 적절한, 올바른
express 표현하다, 나타내다
lawn 잔디
part 부분, 일부
example 예
jog 조깅, 조깅하다
expect 기대하다, 예상하다

We have a test tomorrow.

Pop Quiz Choose and check the right words.

Sally is under a lot of stress.

샐리가 ____________를 많이 받고 있어요.

Dennis doesn't care about the result.

데니스는 ____________에 신경쓰지 않아요.

- ☐ 스트레스
- ☐ 시험
- ☐ 어깨
- ☐ 결과

Catch Up

Listen & Say Listen, say, and color.

Read & Write Write the Basic Words and Jump Up Words.

stress
스트레스, 압박

n

Too much homework causes stress.

너무 많은 숙제는 스트레스의 원인이 돼요.

learn
배우다

v

I'm learning to play the piano.

나는 피아노를 치는 것을 배우고 있어요.

homework
숙제

n

I do my homework.

나는 숙제를 해요.

test
시험

n

They take an English test.

그들은 영어 시험을 봐요.

class
반, 수업

n

We have an art class today.

우리는 오늘 미술 수업이 있어요.

struggle
힘겹게 하다,
허우적거리다

v

Some students may struggle with math.

어떤 학생들은 수학 과목으로 힘겨워할지도 몰라요.

result
결과

n

I got a good result.

나는 좋은 결과를 얻었어요.

shoulder
어깨

n

I put my backpack on my shoulder.

나는 배낭을 어깨에 멨어요.

Skill UP

A Choose and write the words.

test struggle learn

❶ 

배우다

❷ 

시험

❸ 

힘겹게 하다, 허우적거리다

B Cross out, unscramble, and write the words.

❶ 결과 e r l u y s t

❷ 반, 수업 l a s c s t

❸ 어깨 o h s u d b l r e

❹ 스트레스, 압박 s u t e s r s

C Connect and fill in the blanks.

1 

I got a good result.

나는 좋은 __________를 얻었어요.

2 

I put my backpack on my shoulder.

나는 배낭을 __________에 멨어요.

3 

We have an art class today.

우리는 오늘 미술 __________이 있어요.

D Rearrange and write the sentences.

1 나는 숙제를 해요.

do | my | I | homework | .

2 너무 많은 숙제는 스트레스의 원인이 돼요.

stress | Too | much | causes | homework | .

Day 05

Grocery Shopping

Check Up Read and check the words you don't know.

1차 복습

- [ ] stress
- [ ] learn
- [ ] homework
- [ ] test
- [ ] class
- [ ] struggle
- [ ] result
- [ ] shoulder

2차 복습

- [ ] cold
- [ ] revive
- [ ] fever
- [ ] decay

※ **망각 제로!** 1일 전 3일 전 학습한 단어를 복습해요.

Word Tip

stress 스트레스, 압박
class 반, 수업
cold 감기
learn 배우다
struggle 힘겹게 하다, 허우적거리다
revive 회복하다, 활기를 되찾다
homework 숙제
result 결과
fever 열
test 시험
shoulder 어깨
decay 썩다, 부패하다

Pork or beef?

Pop Quiz Choose and check the right words.

Dennis wants both beef and pork.

데니스는 소고기와 돼지고기 ______________ 를 원해요.

- ☐ 둘 다(의)
- ☐ 연약한

Dennis prefers oranges.

데니스는 오렌지______________.

- ☐ ~을 더 좋아하다
- ☐ 회복하다

Catch UP

Listen & Say Listen, say, and color.

Read & Write Write the **Basic Words** and **Jump Up Words.**

pork
돼지고기

n

My family likes to eat pork.

우리 가족은 돼지고기 먹는 것을 좋아해요.

beef
소고기

n

How about buying some beef?

소고기 좀 사는 게 어때요?

bill
계산서

n

I always check my bills.

나는 항상 계산서를 확인해요.

both
둘 다(의)

det

I bought **both** milk and yogurt.

나는 우유와 요구르트를 둘 다 샀어요.

cost
비용, 값

n

The receipt shows the total **cost**.

영수증에는 총비용이 나와 있어요.

prefer
~을 더 좋아하다

v

I **prefer** to buy fresh food.

나는 신선한 음식을 사는 것을 더 좋아해요.

delicate
연약한, 섬세한

a

This cup looks very **delicate**.

이 컵은 매우 연약해 보여요.

advantage
장점, 이점

n

This is one good **advantage** of online shopping.

이것은 온라인 쇼핑의 장점 중 하나예요.

Skill up

A Find, circle, and write the words.

1 

a m c b e e f y

소고기

2 

q w b p o r k m

돼지고기

3 

u b m r t b i l l

계산서

4 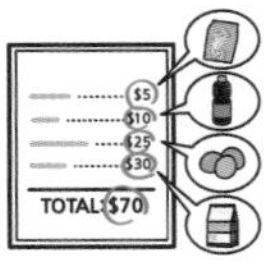

z n c o s t e z

비용, 값

B Choose and write the words.

delicate advantage prefer both

1 둘 다(의)

2 ~을 더 좋아하다

3 연약한, 섬세한

4 장점, 이점

C Connect and fill in the blanks.

1 

I bought both milk and yogurt.
나는 우유와 요구르트를 __________ 샀어요.

2 

I prefer to buy fresh food.
나는 신선한 음식을 사는 것 __________.

3 

This cup looks very delicate.
이 컵은 매우 __________ 보여요.

D Choose and complete the sentences.

bills	cost	beef

1 소고기 좀 사는 게 어때요?

How about buying some __________?

2 나는 항상 계산서를 확인해요.

I always check the __________.

3 영수증에는 총비용이 나와 있어요.

The receipt shows the total __________.

WORD MAZE Follow the correctly spelled words.

Day 01~05

part 부분, 일부	example 예	thing 것, 물건	band 밴드, 그룹	end 끝나다, 끝

aim 목표, 목표하다	jog 조깅, 조깅하다	expect 기대하다, 예상하다	cold 감기	fever 열

health 건강	fine 괜찮은, 좋은	headache 두통	faint 어지러운, 희미한, 기절하다	revive 회복하다, 활기를 되찾다

decay 썩다, 부패하다	thank 감사하다, 고마워하다	sorry 미안한, 안쓰러운	again 다시, 한 번 더	guide 안내하다, 이끌다

letter 편지	proper 적절한, 올바른	express 표현하다, 나타내다	lawn 잔디	stress 스트레스, 압박

learn 배우다	homework 숙제	test 시험	class 반, 수업	struggle 힘겹게 하다, 허우적거리다

result 결과	shoulder 어깨	pork 돼지고기	beef 소고기	bill 계산서

both 둘 다(의)	cost 비용, 값	prefer ~을 더 좋아하다	delicate 연약한, 섬세한	advantage 장점, 이점

Review TEST

맞힌 개수 : ☐ / 40

① part		㉑ 끝나다, 끝	
② example		㉒ 목표, 목표하다	
③ thing		㉓ 조깅, 조깅하다	
④ expect		㉔ 밴드, 그룹	
⑤ cold		㉕ 두통	
⑥ faint		㉖ 열	
⑦ revive		㉗ 건강	
⑧ fine		㉘ 썩다, 부패하다	
⑨ thank		㉙ 편지	
⑩ sorry		㉚ 적절한, 올바른	
⑪ express		㉛ 다시, 한 번 더	
⑫ guide		㉜ 잔디	
⑬ stress		㉝ 반, 수업	
⑭ struggle		㉞ 배우다	
⑮ homework		㉟ 결과	
⑯ test		㊱ 어깨	
⑰ pork		㊲ 비용, 값	
⑱ beef		㊳ ~을 더 좋아하다	
⑲ bill		㊴ 연약한, 섬세한	
⑳ both		㊵ 장점, 이점	

Part 2

Day 06

Geography

Check Up Read and check the words you don't know.

1차 복습

- [ ] pork
- [ ] beef
- [ ] bill
- [ ] both
- [ ] cost
- [ ] prefer
- [ ] delicate
- [ ] advantage

2차 복습

- [ ] thank
- [ ] sorry
- [ ] express
- [ ] lawn

※망각 제로! 1일 전 3일 전 학습한 단어를 복습해요.

Word Tip

pork 돼지고기
beef 소고기
bill 계산서
both 둘 다(의)
cost 비용, 값
prefer ~을 더 좋아하다
delicate 연약한, 섬세한
advantage 장점, 이점
thank 감사하다, 고마워하다
sorry 미안한, 안쓰러운
express 표현하다, 나타내다
lawn 잔디

Let's talk about other countries!

Pop Quiz Choose and check the right words.

There are many countries in the world.

_______________에는 많은 나라들이 있어요.

☐ 세계
☐ 국가

Kiara wants to go to some small towns in the UK.

키아라는 영국의 작은 _______________들에 가고 싶어해요.

☐ 소도시
☐ 장소

Catch Up

Listen & Say Listen, say, and color.

Read & Write Write the Basic Words and Jump Up Words.

world
세계

n

I want to travel all over the world.

나는 전 세계를 여행하고 싶어요.

country
국가, 나라

n

What country are you from?

어느 나라에서 오셨어요?

city
도시

n

I live in the city.

나는 도시에 살아요.

town
소도시, 시내

n

They have dinner in town.
그들은 시내에서 저녁을 먹어요.

place
장소, 곳

n

Here is a good place.
여기는 좋은 곳이에요.

rapid
빠른

a

The river flowed at a rapid pace.
그 강은 빠른 속도로 흘러갔어요.

abundant
풍부한

a

There are abundant trees.
나무가 많이 있어요.

distant
먼, 동떨어진

a

The North Pole is a distant place.
북극은 먼 곳이에요.

Skill UP

A Choose and write the words.

town country distant

1

소도시, 시내

2

먼, 동떨어진

3

국가, 나라

B Choose and write the words.

rapid world place abundant

1 세계

2 풍부한

3 빠른

4 장소, 곳

C Unscramble and complete the sentences.

1 

나는 전 세계를 여행하고 싶어요.

o w r l d

I want to travel all over the ________.

2 

나는 도시에 살아요.

c y t i

I live in the ________.

3 

그 강은 빠른 속도로 흘러갔어요.

r d a p i

The river flowed at a ________ pace.

D Rearrange and write the sentences.

1 어느 나라에서 오셨어요?

you | from | What | country | are | ?

2 나무가 많이 있어요.

There | trees | are | abundant | .

Day 07

Cleaning

Check Up

Read and check the words you don't know.

1차 복습

- [ ] world
- [ ] country
- [ ] city
- [ ] town
- [ ] place
- [ ] rapid
- [ ] abundant
- [ ] distant

2차 복습

- [ ] stress
- [ ] learn
- [ ] result
- [ ] shoulder

3차 복습

- [ ] thing
- [ ] band
- [ ] end
- [ ] aim

※망각 제로! 1일 전 3일 전 7일 전 학습한 단어를 복습해요.

Word Tip

world 세계	country 국가, 나라	city 도시	town 소도시, 시내
place 장소, 곳	rapid 빠른	abundant 풍부한	distant 먼, 동떨어진
stress 스트레스, 압박	learn 배우다	result 결과	shoulder 어깨
thing 것, 물건	band 밴드, 그룹	end 끝나다, 끝	aim 목표, 목표하다

Let's clean the house!

Pop Quiz Choose and check the right words.

Dennis's family cleans their house every weekend.

데니스의 가족은 주말마다 집을 ____________.

☐ 머무르다
☐ 청소하다

Dennis's dad is doing the laundry.

아빠는 ____________을 해요.

☐ 먼지
☐ 세탁

Catch Up

Listen & Say Listen, say, and color.

Read & Write Write the **Basic Words** and **Jump Up Words.**

wash 씻다	I wash my hands. 나는 내 손을 씻어요.
clean 청소하다	I clean my room. 나는 내 방을 청소해요.
wait 기다리다	I'm waiting my turn. 나는 내 차례를 기다리고 있어요.

stay
머무르다

ⓥ I stay at home.
나는 집에 머물러요.

weekend
주말

ⓝ I help my mom on weekends.
나는 주말마다 엄마를 도와요.

recycle
재활용하다

ⓥ I recycle paper, plastic, and cans.
나는 종이, 플라스틱, 캔을 재활용해요.

dust
먼지

ⓝ I wipe the dust off the bookshelf.
나는 선반의 먼지를 닦아요.

laundry
세탁, 세탁물

ⓝ I am doing the laundry.
나는 세탁을 하고 있어요.

Skill UP

A Find, circle, and write the words.

1 

chwaitlp

기다리다

2 

kgdustim

먼지

3 

efcleanf

청소하다

4 

rlaundry

세탁,
세탁물

B Cross out, unscramble, and write the words.

1 재활용하다 eecnylrc

2 주말 keenedcw

3 머무르다 ayust

4 씻다 huswa

C Connect and fill in the blanks.

1 

2 

3 

I help my mom on weekends.
나는 __________마다 엄마를 도와요.

I wash my hands.
나는 내 손을 __________.

I recycle paper, plastic, and cans.
나는 종이, 플라스틱, 캔을 __________.

D Choose and complete the sentences.

laundry   stay   dust

1 나는 집에 머물러요.

I __________ at home.

2 나는 선반의 먼지를 닦아요.

I wipe the __________ off the bookshelf.

3 나는 세탁을 하고 있어요.

I am doing the __________.

Day 08 Positive Qualities

Check Up Read and check the words you don't know.

1차 복습

- [ ] wash
- [ ] clean
- [ ] wait
- [ ] stay
- [ ] weekend
- [ ] recycle
- [ ] dust
- [ ] laundry

2차 복습

- [ ] pork
- [ ] beef
- [ ] delicate
- [ ] advantage

3차 복습

- [ ] health
- [ ] fine
- [ ] headache
- [ ] faint

※망각 제로! 1일 전 3일 전 7일 전 학습한 단어를 복습해요.

Word Tip

wash 씻다	clean 청소하다	wait 기다리다	stay 머무르다
weekend 주말	recycle 재활용하다	dust 먼지	laundry 세탁, 세탁물
pork 돼지고기	beef 소고기	delicate 연약한, 섬세한	advantage 장점, 이점
health 건강	fine 괜찮은, 좋은	headache 두통	faint 어지러운, 희미한, 기절하다

What a handsome boy!

Pop Quiz Choose and check the right words.

Kiara thinks a new student is handsome.

키아라는 전학생이 ____________다고 생각해요.

☐ 잘생긴

☐ 재미있는

Sally said, "He is very honest."

샐리가 전학생이 아주 ____________하다고 말했어요.

☐ 정직한

☐ 우아한

Catch Up

Listen & Say Listen, say, and color.

Read & Write Write the **Basic Words** and **Jump Up Words.**

famous
유명한

The singer is famous.
그 가수는 유명해요.

ⓐ

great
훌륭한, 엄청난

My dad is a great cook.
우리 아빠는 훌륭한 요리사예요.

ⓐ

fun
재미있는

Swimming in the pool is fun.
수영장에서 수영하는 것은 재미있어요.

ⓐ

handsome
잘생긴, 멋진

a

My grandpa was a handsome man.

우리 할아버지는 잘생긴 분이셨어요.

honest
정직한

a

It's important to be honest.

정직해지는 것은 중요해요.

grace
우아함, 품위

n

The dancer moved with grace.

그 무용수는 우아하게 움직였어요.

rare
드문, 희귀한

a

It is rare to find a true friend.

진정한 친구를 찾는 것은 드물어요.

legend
전설적인 인물, 전설

n

My grandpa was a legend.

우리 할아버지는 전설적인 분이셨어요.

Skill UP

A Choose and write the words.

handsome fun grace

1

우아함, 품위

2

재미있는

3

잘생긴, 멋진

B Choose and write the words.

rare honest legend famous

1. 정직한
2. 전설적인 인물, 전설
3. 유명한
4. 드문, 희귀한

C Unscramble and complete the sentences.

1 

우리 아빠는 훌륭한 요리사예요.

r e a g t

My dad is a ________ cook.

2 

그 가수는 유명해요.

a u f o m s

The singer is ________.

3 

정직해지는 것은 중요해요.

h e o s t n

It's important to be ________.

D Rearrange and write the sentences.

1 수영장에서 수영하는 것은 재미있어요.

in | Swimming | fun | the pool | is | .

2 우리 할아버지는 전설적인 분이셨어요.

My | a legend | was | grandpa | .

Day 09 Jobs

Check Up Read and check the words you don't know.

1차 복습

- [ ] famous
- [ ] great
- [ ] fun
- [ ] handsome
- [ ] honest
- [ ] grace
- [ ] rare
- [ ] legend

2차 복습

- [ ] world
- [ ] country
- [ ] abundant
- [ ] distant

3차 복습

- [ ] again
- [ ] guide
- [ ] letter
- [ ] proper

※망각 제로! 1일 전 3일 전 7일 전 학습한 단어를 복습해요.

Word Tip

famous 유명한
honest 정직한
world 세계
again 다시, 한 번 더

great 훌륭한, 엄청난
grace 우아함, 품위
country 국가, 나라
guide 안내하다, 이끌다

fun 재미있는
rare 드문, 희귀한
abundant 풍부한
letter 편지

handsome 잘생긴, 멋진
legend 전설적인 인물, 전설
distant 먼, 동떨어진
proper 적절한, 올바른

I am a dentist.

Pop Quiz Choose and check the right words.

Kiara is a dentist.

키아라는 ____________ 예요.

Rod's dream is to be a firefighter.

로드의 ____________ 은 소방관이에요.

☐ 치과 의사

☐ 경찰

☐ 가치

☐ 꿈

Catch Up

Listen & Say Listen, say, and color.

Read & Write Write the **Basic Words** and **Jump Up Words.**

work
일하다, 일

v n

He goes to work at 8.

그는 8시에 일하러 가요.

dentist
치과 의사

n

My dad is a dentist.

우리 아빠는 치과 의사예요.

police
경찰

n

Someone call the police!

누가 경찰을 불러 주세요!

grow 재배하다, 자라다	ⓥ **Farmers grow crops.** 농부는 농작물을 재배해요. 
dream 꿈, 꿈꾸다	ⓝ ⓥ **My dream is to be an artist.** 나의 꿈은 예술가예요. 
value 가치	ⓝ **Teamwork is an important value to me.** 팀워크는 나에게 중요한 가치예요. 
arrest 체포하다	ⓥ **The police officer arrested the suspect.** 경찰관은 용의자를 체포했어요. 
invest 투자하다	ⓥ **My parents invest money well.** 나의 부모님은 돈 투자를 잘하세요. 

Skill UP

A Choose and write the words.

work　　arrest　　grow

❶ 

일하다, 일

❷ 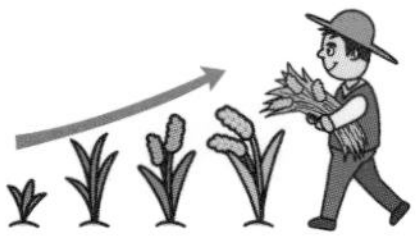

재배하다, 자라다

❸ 

체포하다

B Cross out, unscramble, and write the words.

❶ 꿈, 꿈꾸다　d a e r n m

❷ 치과 의사　t e n d s t b i

❸ 가치　a y v u e l

❹ 투자하다　e s i v t r n

C Connect and fill in the blanks.

1 

2 

3 

My dad is a dentist.
우리 아빠는 ____________ 예요.

Someone call the police!
누가 ____________ 을 불러 주세요!

My dream is to be an artist.
나의 ____________ 은 예술가예요.

D Choose and complete the sentences.

invest	work	value

1 그는 8시에 일하러 가요.

He goes to ____________ at 8.

2 나의 부모님은 돈 투자를 잘하세요.

My parents ____________ money well.

3 팀워크는 나에게 중요한 가치예요.

Teamwork is an important ____________ to me.

Day 10 Communication

Check Up Read and check the words you don't know.

1차 복습

- [ ] work
- [ ] dentist
- [ ] police
- [ ] grow
- [ ] dream
- [ ] value
- [ ] arrest
- [ ] invest

2차 복습

- [ ] wash
- [ ] clean
- [ ] dust
- [ ] laundry

3차 복습

- [ ] homework
- [ ] test
- [ ] class
- [ ] struggle

※망각 제로! 1일 전 3일 전 7일 전 학습한 단어를 복습해요.

Word Tip

work 일하다, 일	dentist 치과 의사	police 경찰	grow 재배하다, 자라다
dream 꿈, 꿈꾸다	value 가치	arrest 체포하다	invest 투자하다
wash 씻다	clean 청소하다	dust 먼지	laundry 세탁, 세탁물
homework 숙제	test 시험	class 반, 수업	struggle 힘겹게 하다, 허우적거리다

Grandmother tells me interesting stories.

Pop Quiz Choose and check the right words.

Dennis welcomes his grandmother.

데니스는 할머니를 반갑게 ____________.

☐ 예측하다

☐ 맞이하다

Dennis likes his grandmother's stories.

데니스는 할머니의 ____________를 좋아해요.

☐ 이야기

☐ 질문

Catch Up

Listen & Say Listen, say, and color.

Read & Write Write the **Basic Words** and **Jump Up Words.**

because
~ 때문에

conj

I was late because the traffic was bad.

나는 차가 많이 막혔기 때문에 늦었어요.

question
질문

n

Do you have any questions?

질문 있나요?

talk
말하다

v

We talk to each other.

우리는 서로에게 말해요.

welcome 맞이하다, 환영하다 (v)

My grandma welcomes me.

우리 할머니는 나를 맞이해 주세요.

story 이야기 (n)

She told me a story.

그녀는 나에게 이야기를 해 주었어요.

reply 답장을 보내다, 대답하다 (v)

He replied to my e-mail.

그는 내 이메일에 답장했어요.

predict 예측하다 (v)

Scientists can predict earthquakes.

과학자들은 지진을 예측할 수 있어요.

intend (~하려고) 생각하다, 의도하다 (v)

I intend to clean my room.

나는 내 방을 청소할 생각이에요.

Skill UP

A Choose and write the words.

reply　　question　　welcome

1 

질문

2 

맞이하다, 환영하다

3 

답장을 보내다, 대답하다

B Choose and write the words.

because　　intend　　predict　　story

1 (~하려고) 생각하다, 의도하다

2 예측하다

3 이야기

4 ~ 때문에

C Unscramble and complete the sentences.

1 

우리는 서로에게 말해요.

a l k t

We ________ to each other.

2 

나는 내 방을 청소할 생각이에요.

t d e i n n

I ________ to clean my room.

3 

그녀는 나에게 이야기를 해 주었어요.

r s o y t

She told me a ________ .

D Rearrange and write the sentences.

1 과학자들은 지진을 예측할 수 있어요.

Scientists | earthquakes | can | predict | .

2 그는 내 이메일에 답장했어요.

to | replied | He | e-mail | my | .

WORD SEARCH Find, circle, and write the words.

Words go in 2 directions → ↓

r	z	v	x	m	c	d	b	p	u	o	u	y	g	h
y	x	p	n	m	u	e	f	t	t	f	p	z	q	r
l	n	d	o	g	p	n	u	c	w	x	b	z	g	e
e	u	l	f	y	e	t	n	p	o	l	i	c	e	c
g	r	a	c	e	s	i	o	s	l	p	q	s	v	y
m	a	t	o	w	n	s	o	l	c	y	c	t	y	c
l	f	e	z	x	t	t	z	t	a	l	k	o	b	l
q	t	q	s	x	z	p	e	n	q	c	a	r	q	e
c	i	t	y	z	y	k	u	z	d	a	d	y	j	x
l	p	j	l	c	l	e	a	n	y	s	w	u	k	i

Word Bank

town
city
clean
recycle
grace
fun
dentist
police
talk
story

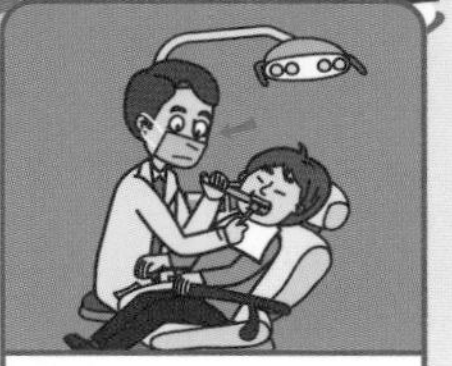

dentist

world 세계	country 국가, 나라	city 도시	town 소도시, 시내	place 장소, 곳

rapid 빠른	abundant 풍부한	distant 먼, 동떨어진	wash 씻다	clean 청소하다

wait 기다리다	stay 머무르다	weekend 주말	recycle 재활용하다	dust 먼지

laundry 세탁, 세탁물	famous 유명한	great 훌륭한, 엄청난	fun 재미있는	handsome 잘생긴, 멋진

honest 정직한	grace 우아함, 품위	rare 드문, 희귀한	legend 전설적인 인물, 전설	work 일하다, 일

dentist 치과 의사	police 경찰	grow 재배하다, 자라다	dream 꿈, 꿈꾸다	value 가치

arrest 체포하다	invest 투자하다	because ~ 때문에	question 질문	talk 말하다

welcome 맞이하다, 환영하다	story 이야기	reply 답장을 보내다, 대답하다	predict 예측하다	intend (~하려고) 생각하다, 의도하다

Review TEST

맞힌 개수 : [ ] /40

① world		㉑ 장소, 곳	
② country		㉒ 빠른	
③ city		㉓ 풍부한	
④ town		㉔ 먼, 동떨어진	
⑤ wash		㉕ 주말	
⑥ clean		㉖ 재활용하다	
⑦ wait		㉗ 먼지	
⑧ stay		㉘ 세탁, 세탁물	
⑨ famous		㉙ 정직한	
⑩ great		㉚ 우아함, 품위	
⑪ fun		㉛ 드문, 희귀한	
⑫ legend		㉜ 잘생긴, 멋진	
⑬ work		㉝ 꿈, 꿈꾸다	
⑭ dentist		㉞ 가치	
⑮ police		㉟ 체포하다	
⑯ grow		㊱ 투자하다	
⑰ because		㊲ 이야기	
⑱ reply		㊳ 질문	
⑲ intend		㊴ 예측하다	
⑳ welcome		㊵ 말하다	

Part 3

Day 11

Daily Routines

Check Up Read and check the words you don't know.

1차 복습

- [ ] because
- [ ] question
- [ ] talk
- [ ] welcome
- [ ] story
- [ ] reply
- [ ] predict
- [ ] intend

2차 복습

- [ ] famous
- [ ] great
- [ ] rare
- [ ] legend

3차 복습

- [ ] bill
- [ ] both
- [ ] cost
- [ ] prefer

※망각 제로! 1일 전 3일 전 7일 전 학습한 단어를 복습해요.

Word Tip

because ~ 때문에	**question** 질문	**talk** 말하다	**welcome** 맞이하다, 환영하다
story 이야기	**reply** 답장을 보내다, 대답하다	**predict** 예측하다	**intend** (~하려고) 생각하다, 의도하다
famous 유명한	**great** 훌륭한, 엄청난	**rare** 드문, 희귀한	**legend** 전설적인 인물, 전설
bill 계산서	**both** 둘 다(의)	**cost** 비용, 값	**prefer** ~을 더 좋아하다

How about strawberry curry?

Pop Quiz Choose and check the right words.

There is food on the table.

________에 음식이 있어요.

☐ 식탁

☐ 식사

Rod's mom left a note.

로드의 엄마가 ________를 남겼어요.

☐ 메모

☐ 붓

Catch Up

Listen & Say Listen, say, and color.

Read & Write Write the **Basic Words** and **Jump Up Words.**

brush
붓, 솔질하다

n v

I clean my **brush**.
나는 붓을 닦아요.

note
메모, 쪽지

n

She wrote a **note** in her book.
그녀는 책에 메모를 적었어요.

table
식탁, 탁자

n

I like to keep my **table** clean.
나는 식탁을 깨끗하게 유지하는 것을 좋아해요.

meal
식사, 끼니

n

We have three meals a day.

우리는 하루에 세 끼를 먹어요.

strawberry
딸기

n

There is a strawberry on the cake.

케이크 위에 딸기가 있어요.

review
검토하다,
복습하다

v

I need to review my homework.

나는 숙제를 검토해야 해요.

spend
(시간을) 보내다,
(돈을) 쓰다

v

I usually spend an hour at the gym.

나는 보통 체육관에서 한 시간을 보내요.

curry
카레

n

I often eat curry for dinner.

나는 저녁으로 카레를 자주 먹어요.

Skill UP

A Find, circle, and write the words.

1 

abrushfm

붓, 솔질하다

2 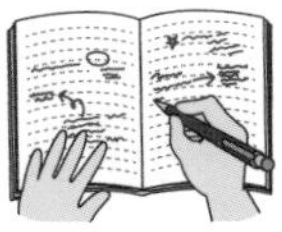

qwbnotez

메모, 쪽지

3 

nmealkgy

식사, 끼니

4 

tablemao

식탁, 탁자

B Cross out, unscramble, and write the words.

1 카레 — cauyrr

2 (시간을) 보내다, (돈을) 쓰다 — despin

3 검토하다, 복습하다 — eyriewv

4 식사, 끼니 — elarm

C Connect and fill in the blanks.

❶ 

I need to review my homework.

나는 숙제를 ____________야 해요.

❷ 

I usually spend an hour at the gym.

나는 보통 체육관에서 한 시간을 ____________.

❸ 

I often eat curry for dinner.

나는 저녁으로 ____________를 자주 먹어요.

D Choose and complete the sentences.

brush note strawberry

❶ 나는 붓을 닦아요.

I clean my ____________.

❷ 케이크 위에 딸기가 있어요.

There is a ____________ on the cake.

❸ 그녀는 책에 메모를 적었어요.

She wrote a ____________ in her book.

Day 12 Travel

Check Up Read and check the words you don't know.

1차 복습

- [ ] brush
- [ ] note
- [ ] table
- [ ] meal
- [ ] strawberry
- [ ] review
- [ ] spend
- [ ] curry

2차 복습

- [ ] work
- [ ] dentist
- [ ] arrest
- [ ] invest

3차 복습

- [ ] city
- [ ] town
- [ ] place
- [ ] rapid

※**망각 제로!** 1일 전 3일 전 7일 전 학습한 단어를 복습해요.

Word Tip

brush 붓, 솔질하다
strawberry 딸기
work 일하다, 일
city 도시

note 메모, 쪽지
review 검토하다, 복습하다
dentist 치과 의사
town 소도시, 시내

table 식탁, 탁자
spend (시간을) 보내다, (돈을) 쓰다
arrest 체포하다
place 장소, 곳

meal 식사, 끼니
curry 카레
invest 투자하다
rapid 빠른

Where do you want to go?

Pop Quiz Choose and check the right words.

Sally wants to visit an ancient city.

샐리는 ____________ 도시를 방문하고 싶어해요.

☐ 고대의

☐ 풍습

Kiara likes exotic places.

키아라는 ____________ 곳을 좋아해요.

☐ 이국적인

☐ 바다

Catch Up

Listen & Say Listen, say, and color.

Read & Write Write the **Basic Words** and **Jump Up Words.**

sea 바다	n I saw the most beautiful sea. 나는 가장 아름다운 바다를 보았어요.
tower 탑	n We climbed to the top of the tower. 우리는 탑의 꼭대기에 올라갔어요.
weather 날씨	n The weather is perfect for the beach. 해변에 가기에 완벽한 날씨예요.

holiday
휴일

n

Thanksgiving Day is a **holiday**.
추수감사절은 휴일이에요.

airport
공항

n

We arrived at the **airport**.
우리는 공항에 도착했어요.

custom
풍습, 관습

n

We followed the local **custom**.
우리는 그 지역의 풍습을 따랐어요.

exotic
외국의,
이국적인

a

I love **exotic** fruits.
나는 외국 과일을 좋아해요.

ancient
고대의,
아주 오래된

a

I visited an **ancient** mosque.
나는 고대 모스크를 방문했어요.

Skill UP

A Choose and write the words.

weather　　exotic　　airport

1 

공항

2 

날씨

3 

외국의, 이국적인

B Choose and write the words.

sea　　custom　　ancient　　holiday

1 휴일

2 고대의, 아주 오래된

3 풍습, 관습

4 바다

C Connect and fill in the blanks.

1 

2 

3 

We climbed to the top of the tower.

우리는 __________의 꼭대기에 올라갔어요.

Thanksgiving Day is a holiday.

추수감사절은 __________이에요.

I visited an ancient mosque.

나는 __________ 모스크를 방문했어요.

D Rearrange and write the sentences.

1 우리는 공항에 도착했어요.

We | at | arrived | the airport | .

____

2 나는 외국 과일을 좋아해요.

love | exotic | I | fruits | .

____

Day 13

Time & Habits

Check Up

Read and check the words you don't know.

1차 복습

- [ ] sea
- [ ] tower
- [ ] weather
- [ ] holiday
- [ ] airport
- [ ] custom
- [ ] exotic
- [ ] ancient

2차 복습

- [ ] because
- [ ] question
- [ ] predict
- [ ] intend

3차 복습

- [ ] wait
- [ ] stay
- [ ] weekend
- [ ] recycle

※망각 제로! 1일 전 3일 전 7일 전 학습한 단어를 복습해요.

Word Tip

sea 바다
tower 탑
weather 날씨
holiday 휴일
airport 공항
custom 풍습, 관습
exotic 외국의, 이국적인
ancient 고대의, 아주 오래된
because ~ 때문에
question 질문
predict 예측하다
intend (~하려고) 생각하다, 의도하다
wait 기다리다
stay 머무르다
weekend 주말
recycle 재활용하다

It's hard to wake up early.

Pop Quiz Choose and check the right words.

Kiara is late again.

키아라는 또 ___________.

☐ 이른

☐ 늦은

Dennis recommends that Kiara sleep with her clothes on.

데니스는 키아라에게 옷을 입고 자는 것을 ___________.

☐ 추천하다

☐ 노력하다

Catch Up

Listen & Say Listen, say, and color.

Read & Write Write the **Basic Words** and **Jump Up Words.**

wake
깨우다,
(잠에서) 깨다

v

The birds wake me up in the morning.

새들이 아침에 나를 깨워요.

early
일찍, 이른

adv a

I wake up early in the morning.

나는 아침에 일찍 일어나요.

late
늦은, 늦게

a adv

I'm sometimes late for school.

나는 가끔 학교에 늦어요.

always
항상

adv

He **always** eats vegetables.

그는 항상 채소를 먹어요.

try
노력하다, 시도하다

v

I will **try** to sleep earlier.

나는 좀 더 일찍 자려고 노력할 거예요.

recommend
추천하다

v

I **recommend** drinking water in the morning.

나는 아침에 물을 마시는 것을 추천해요.

ordinary
평범한, 보통의

a

Today is an **ordinary** day.

오늘은 평범한 날이에요.

opinion
생각, 의견

n

In my **opinion**, reading before bed is a good idea.

내 생각에, 자기 전에 책을 읽는 것은 좋은 생각이에요.

Skill UP

A Choose and write the words.

wake recommend late

1 

늦은, 늦게

2 

깨우다, (잠에서) 깨다

3 

추천하다

B Cross out, unscramble, and write the words.

1 일찍, 이른 — r a l e w y

2 항상 — l a w y s a i

3 평범한, 보통의 — a n r d y v i r o

4 노력하다, 시도하다 — t e y r

C Unscramble and complete the sentences.

1 

나는 아침에 일찍 일어나요. **areyl**

I wake up ________ in the morning.

2 

그는 항상 채소를 먹어요. **walysa**

He ________ eats vegetables.

3 

내 생각에, 자기 전에 책을 읽는 것은 좋은 생각이에요. **ionpion**

In my ________, reading before bed is a good idea.

D Rearrange and write the sentences.

1 나는 가끔 학교에 늦어요.

I'm | school | sometimes late | for | .

2 나는 좀 더 일찍 자려고 노력할 거예요.

sleep | will | I | try | to | earlier | .

Day 14

Actions

Check Up Read and check the words you don't know.

1차 복습

- [ ] wake
- [ ] early
- [ ] late
- [ ] always
- [ ] try
- [ ] recommend
- [ ] ordinary
- [ ] opinion

2차 복습

- [ ] brush
- [ ] note
- [ ] spend
- [ ] curry

3차 복습

- [ ] fun
- [ ] handsome
- [ ] honest
- [ ] grace

※망각 제로! 1일 전 3일 전 7일 전 학습한 단어를 복습해요.

Word Tip

wake 깨우다, (잠에서) 깨다
early 일찍, 이른
late 늦은, 늦게
always 항상
try 노력하다, 시도하다
recommend 추천하다
ordinary 평범한, 보통의
opinion 생각, 의견
brush 붓, 솔질하다
note 메모, 쪽지
spend (시간을) 보내다, (돈을) 쓰다
curry 카레
fun 재미있는
handsome 잘생긴, 멋진
honest 정직한
grace 우아함, 품위

What are you busy with?

Pop Quiz Choose and check the right words.

Rod and Dennis look busy.

로드와 데니스는 ____________ 보여요.

☐ 바쁜
☐ 옳은

Mong will fix the drone for them.

몽은 로드와 데니스를 위해 드론을 ____________ 줄 거예요.

☐ 고치다
☐ 싸우다

Catch Up

Listen & Say Listen, say, and color.

Read & Write Write the **Basic Words** and **Jump Up Words.**

busy
바쁜

He is busy now.
그는 지금 바빠요.

right
옳은, 올바른

You were right about the movie.
그 영화에 대해서는 당신이 옳았어요.

wrong
잘못된, 틀린

It's wrong to cheat on a test.
시험에서 부정행위를 하는 건 잘못된 것이에요.

fight
싸우다

We shouldn't fight with friends.
우리는 친구들과 싸우면 안 돼요.

fix
고치다

I need to fix my bike.
나는 자전거를 고쳐야 해요.

prove
증명하다

I can prove it.
나는 그것을 증명할 수 있어요.

accuse
비난하다,
고발하다

Don't accuse me.
나를 비난하지 마세요.

notice
알아채다,
~을 의식하다

I noticed him cheating.
나는 그가 부정행위 하는 것을 알아챘어요.

Skill UP

A Find, circle, and write the words.

1 

싸우다

z p f i g h t k

2 

바쁜

s a b u s y t z

3 

고치다

n m e a f i x y

4 

알아채다,
~을 의식하다

p n o t i c e o

B Choose and write the words.

wrong　right　prove　accuse

1 비난하다, 고발하다

2 옳은, 올바른

3 잘못된, 틀린

4 증명하다

C Unscramble and complete the sentences.

1 

그 영화에 대해서는 당신이 옳았어요.

i g h r t

You were ________ about the movie.

2 

시험에서 부정행위를 하는 건 잘못된 것이에요.

w r n g o

It's ________ to cheat on a test.

3 

나를 비난하지 마세요.

u a c c s e

Don't ________ me.

D Choose and complete the sentences.

prove fix fight

1 나는 그것을 증명할 수 있어요.

I can ________ it.

2 우리는 친구들과 싸우면 안 돼요.

We shouldn't ________ with friends.

3 나는 자전거를 고쳐야 해요.

I need to ________ my bike.

Day 15

Time & Dates

Check Up

Read and check the words you don't know.

1차 복습

- [ ] busy
- [ ] right
- [ ] wrong
- [ ] fight
- [ ] fix
- [ ] prove
- [ ] accuse
- [ ] notice

2차 복습

- [ ] sea
- [ ] tower
- [ ] exotic
- [ ] ancient

3차 복습

- [ ] police
- [ ] grow
- [ ] dream
- [ ] value

※ 망각 제로! 1일 전 3일 전 7일 전 학습한 단어를 복습해요.

Word Tip

busy 바쁜	right 옳은, 올바른	wrong 잘못된, 틀린	fight 싸우다
fix 고치다	prove 증명하다	accuse 비난하다, 고발하다	notice 알아채다, ~을 의식하다
sea 바다	tower 탑	exotic 외국의, 이국적인	ancient 고대의, 아주 오래된
police 경찰	grow 재배하다, 자라다	dream 꿈, 꿈꾸다	value 가치

What is the date today?

Pop Quiz Choose and check the right words.

Instead of a birthday gift, Rod bought Dennis lunch.

로드는 생일 선물 ______________ 점심을 샀어요.

☐ 대신에
☐ 짧은

Dennis's birthday is next month.

데니스의 생일은 다음 ______________ 이에요.

☐ 달, 월
☐ 해, 년

Catch Up

Listen & Say Listen, say, and color.

Read & Write Write the **Basic Words** and **Jump Up Words.**

time
시간

It's time for lunch.
점심 먹을 시간이에요.

year
해, 년

The year is almost over.
한 해가 거의 끝나가요.

month
달, 월

My birthday is next month.
내 생일은 다음 달이에요.

date
날짜

n

What's the date today?

오늘 날짜는 며칠이에요?

day
하루, 날, 요일

n

Have a nice day.

좋은 하루 보내세요.

brief
짧은, 간단한

a

We had a brief chat.

우리는 짧은 이야기를 나눴어요.

instead
대신에

adv

I will leave at night instead.

나는 대신 밤에 출발할 거예요.

past
과거, 지나간

n a

In the past, people used sundials to tell time.

과거에, 사람들은 시간을 말하기 위해 해시계를 사용했어요.

Skill UP

A Choose and write the words.

date　　time　　past

1 

시간

2 

날짜

3 

과거, 지나간

B Cross out, unscramble, and write the words.

1 짧은, 간단한　　r i g e f b

2 하루, 날, 요일　　a y h d

3 달, 월　　a o m h t n

4 대신에　　s n v i e d t a

C Unscramble and complete the sentences.

1 

한 해가 거의 끝나가요.

e y r a

The __________ is almost over.

2 

우리는 짧은 이야기를 나눴어요.

r i b f e

We had a __________ chat.

3 

내 생일은 다음 달이에요.

o m h t n

My birthday is next __________.

D Rearrange and write the sentences.

1 점심 먹을 시간이에요.

time | It's | for | lunch | .

2 오늘 날짜는 며칠이에요?

the date | What's | today | ?

WORD PUZZLE Complete the word puzzle.

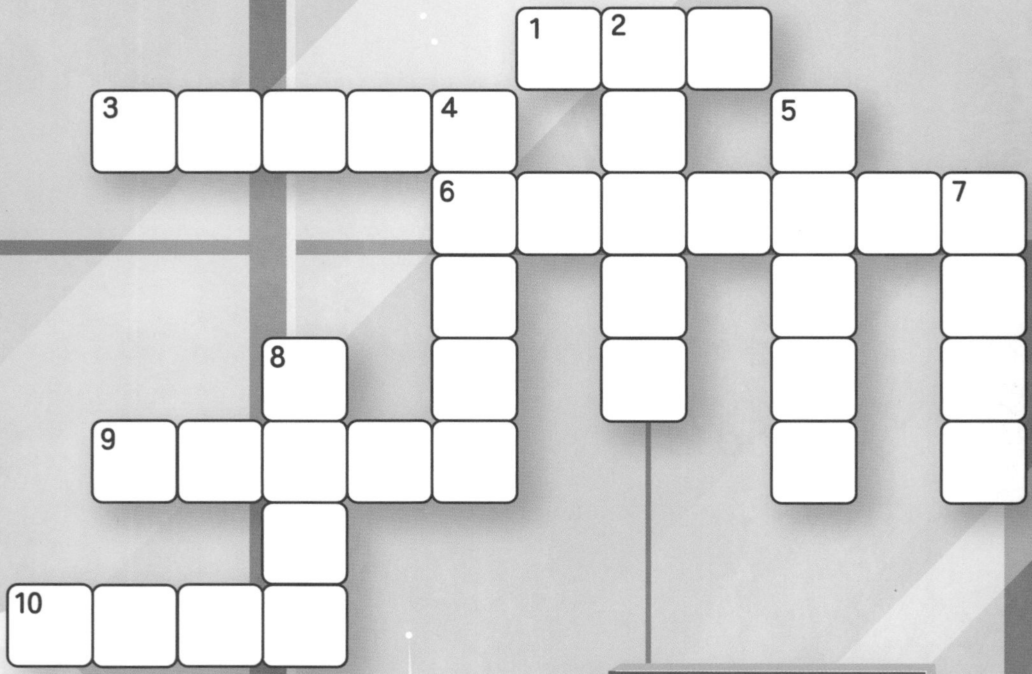

Word Bank

- note
- table
- sea
- airport
- late
- early
- right
- prove
- time
- month

→ ACROSS →

①

③

⑥

⑨

⑩

↓ DOWN ↓

②

④

⑤

⑦

⑧

Day 11~15

brush	**note**	**table**	**meal**	**strawberry**
붓, 솔질하다	메모, 쪽지	식탁, 탁자	식사, 끼니	딸기

review	**spend**	**curry**	**sea**	**tower**
검토하다, 복습하다	(시간을) 보내다, (돈을) 쓰다	카레	바다	탑

weather	**holiday**	**airport**	**custom**	**exotic**
날씨	휴일	공항	풍습, 관습	외국의, 이국적인

ancient	**wake**	**early**	**late**	**always**
고대의, 아주 오래된	깨우다, (잠에서) 깨다	일찍, 이른	늦은, 늦게	항상

try	**recommend**	**ordinary**	**opinion**	**busy**
노력하다, 시도하다	추천하다	평범한, 보통의	생각, 의견	바쁜

right	**wrong**	**fight**	**fix**	**prove**
옳은, 올바른	잘못된, 틀린	싸우다	고치다	증명하다

accuse	**notice**	**time**	**year**	**month**
비난하다, 고발하다	알아채다, ~을 의식하다	시간	해, 년	달, 월

date	**day**	**brief**	**instead**	**past**
날짜	하루, 날, 요일	짧은, 간단한	대신에	과거, 지나간

Review TEST

맞힌 개수 : ☐ / 40

① brush		㉑ 딸기	
② review		㉒ 메모, 쪽지	
③ spend		㉓ 식탁, 탁자	
④ meal		㉔ 카레	
⑤ sea		㉕ 공항	
⑥ tower		㉖ 풍습, 관습	
⑦ weather		㉗ 외국의, 이국적인	
⑧ ancient		㉘ 휴일	
⑨ wake		㉙ 늦은, 늦게	
⑩ early		㉚ 추천하다	
⑪ try		㉛ 평범한, 보통의	
⑫ always		㉜ 생각, 의견	
⑬ busy		㉝ 고치다	
⑭ accuse		㉞ 증명하다	
⑮ wrong		㉟ 옳은, 올바른	
⑯ notice		㊱ 싸우다	
⑰ time		㊲ 하루, 날, 요일	
⑱ year		㊳ 짧은, 간단한	
⑲ month		㊴ 대신에	
⑳ date		㊵ 과거, 지나간	

Part 4

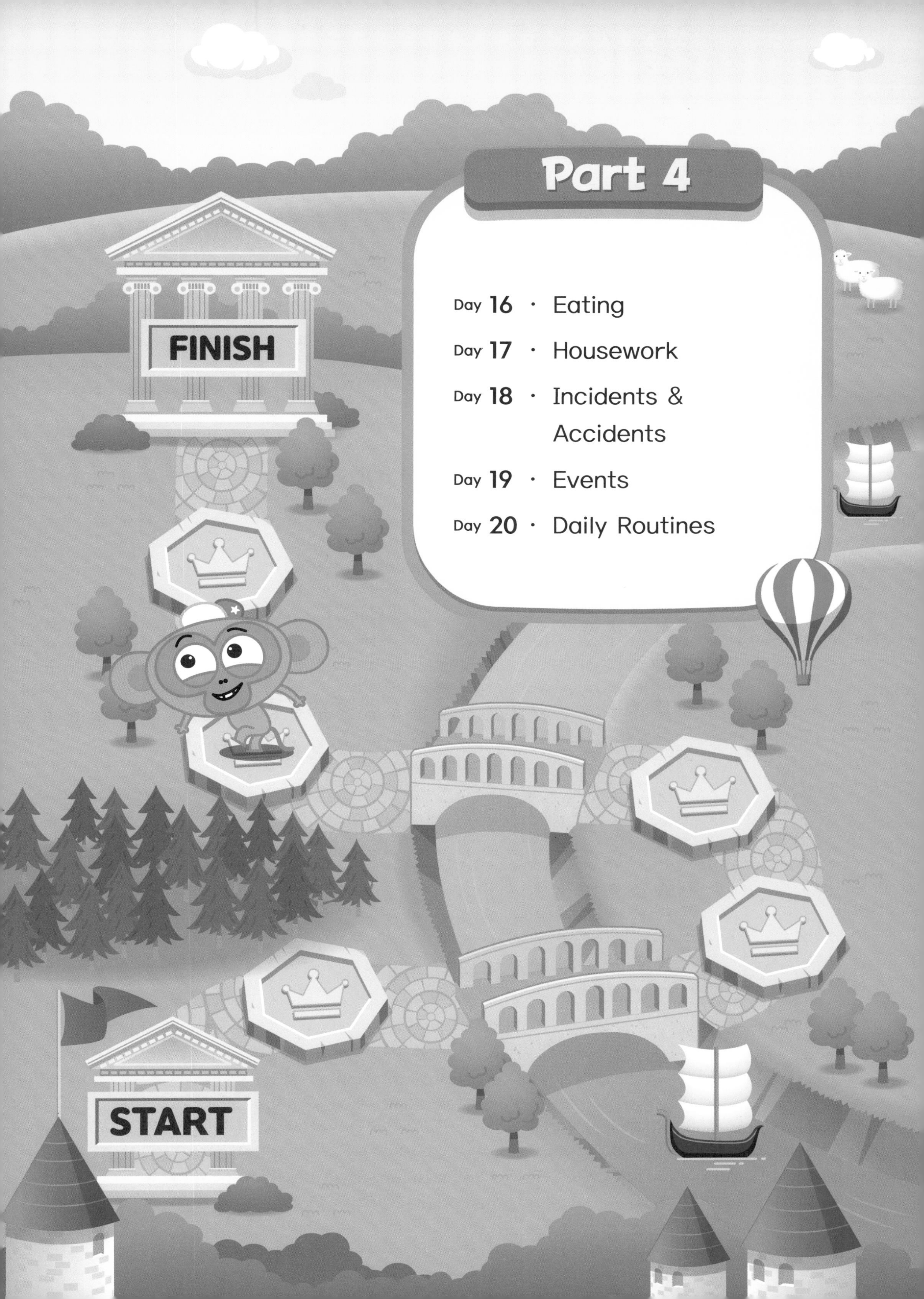

Day 16

Eating

Check Up Read and check the words you don't know.

1차 복습

- [ ] time
- [ ] year
- [ ] month
- [ ] date
- [ ] day
- [ ] brief
- [ ] instead
- [ ] past

2차 복습

- [ ] wake
- [ ] early
- [ ] ordinary
- [ ] opinion

3차 복습

- [ ] talk
- [ ] welcome
- [ ] story
- [ ] reply

※망각 제로! 1일 전 3일 전 7일 전 학습한 단어를 복습해요.

Word Tip

time 시간	year 해, 년	month 달, 월	date 날짜
day 하루, 날, 요일	brief 짧은, 간단한	instead 대신에	past 과거, 지나간
wake 깨우다, (잠에서) 깨다	early 일찍, 이른	ordinary 평범한, 보통의	opinion 생각, 의견
talk 말하다	welcome 맞이하다, 환영하다	story 이야기	reply 답장을 보내다, 대답하다

I have bananas for breakfast.

Pop Quiz Choose and check the right words.

The park is the perfect picnic spot.

공원은 완벽한 소풍 ____________예요.

☐ 장소

☐ 소풍

Mong thinks about what to have for dinner.

몽은 ____________로 무엇을 먹을지 생각 중이에요.

☐ 점심 식사

☐ 저녁 식사

Catch Up

Listen & Say Listen, say, and color.

Read & Write Write the Basic Words and Jump Up Words.

breakfast
아침 식사

n

I have breakfast every day.

나는 매일 아침을 먹어요.

lunch
점심 식사

n

I have lunch with my friends.

나는 친구들과 점심을 먹어요.

dinner
저녁 식사

n

My family has dinner together.

우리 가족은 함께 저녁을 먹어요.

picnic
소풍

n

I packed the food for the picnic.

나는 소풍을 위한 음식을 챙겼어요.

quick
빠른

a

I am a quick eater.

나는 빨리 먹는 사람이에요.

spot
장소

n

This restaurant is a great spot.

이 식당은 아주 좋은 장소예요.

approve
찬성하다

v

I approve of her meal choices.

나는 그녀의 메뉴 선택에 찬성해요.

perfect
완벽한

a

This pizza is perfect!

이 피자는 완벽해요!

Skill UP

A Choose and write the words.

dinner	breakfast	lunch

❶ 

아침 식사

❷ 

점심 식사

❸ 

저녁 식사

B Choose and write the words.

quick	approve	perfect	picnic

❶ 소풍

❷ 완벽한

❸ 찬성하다

❹ 빠른

C Connect and fill in the blanks.

1 

2 

3 

This pizza is perfect!

이 피자는 ____________ 요!

I approve of her meal choices.

나는 그녀의 메뉴 선택에 ____________.

I packed the food for the picnic.

나는 ____________ 을 위한 음식을 챙겼어요.

D Choose and complete the sentences.

spot	dinner	breakfast

1 우리 가족은 함께 저녁을 먹어요.

My family has ____________ together.

2 나는 매일 아침을 먹어요.

I have ____________ every day.

3 이 식당은 아주 좋은 장소예요.

This restaurant is a great ____________.

Day 17 Housework

Check Up Read and check the words you don't know.

1차 복습

- [ ] breakfast
- [ ] lunch
- [ ] dinner
- [ ] picnic
- [ ] quick
- [ ] spot
- [ ] approve
- [ ] perfect

2차 복습

- [ ] busy
- [ ] right
- [ ] accuse
- [ ] notice

3차 복습

- [ ] table
- [ ] meal
- [ ] strawberry
- [ ] review

※망각 제로! 1일 전 3일 전 7일 전 학습한 단어를 복습해요.

Word Tip

breakfast 아침 식사
lunch 점심 식사
dinner 저녁 식사
picnic 소풍
quick 빠른
spot 장소
approve 찬성하다
perfect 완벽한
busy 바쁜
right 옳은, 올바른
accuse 비난하다, 고발하다
notice 알아채다, ~을 의식하다
table 식탁, 탁자
meal 식사, 끼니
strawberry 딸기
review 검토하다, 복습하다

She enjoys cleaning!

Pop Quiz Choose and check the right words.

Dennis invented an automatic cleaner.

데니스는 ____________ 청소기를 발명했어요.

☐ 더러운

☐ 자동의

Lily enjoys using the automatic cleaner.

릴리는 자동 청소기 사용을 ____________.

☐ 즐기다

☐ 발명하다

Catch Up

Listen & Say Listen, say, and color.

Read & Write Write the **Basic Words** and **Jump Up Words.**

home
집

n

I clean my home every weekend.
나는 주말마다 집을 청소해요.

dirty
더러운

a

I mopped the dirty floor.
나는 더러운 바닥을 닦았어요.

shower
샤워를 하다

v

I showered after cleaning the house.
나는 집을 청소한 후에 샤워했어요.

enjoy
즐기다

v

I enjoy washing my car.
나는 세차하는 것을 즐겨요.

often
자주, 흔히

adv

I often do the laundry on weekdays.
나는 평일에 자주 빨래해요.

automatic
자동의

a

My dishwasher is automatic.
나의 식기세척기는 자동이에요.

machine
기계

n

I use the washing machine.
나는 세탁기를 사용해요.

invent
발명하다

v

My dad invented a new cleaning tool.
우리 아빠는 새로운 청소 도구를 발명했어요.

Skill UP

A Find, circle, and write the words.

1 

집

m z p f h o m e

2 

샤워를 하다

s f s h o w e r

3 

발명하다

n i n v e n t m

4 

기계

b m a c h i n e

B Cross out, unscramble, and write the words.

1 자동의 u f a t m t c i o a

2 더러운 r d y g i t

3 즐기다 e y n o j h

4 자주, 흔히 s f t n o e

C Unscramble and complete the sentences.

1 

나는 더러운 바닥을 닦았어요.

i d r y t

I mopped the __________ floor.

2 

나는 세차하는 것을 즐겨요.

e y n o j

I __________ washing my car.

3 

나의 식기세척기는 자동이에요.

u a o t m a i c t

My dishwasher is __________.

D Choose and complete the sentences.

often machine home

1 나는 주말마다 집을 청소해요.

I clean my __________ every weekend.

2 나는 세탁기를 사용해요.

I use the washing __________.

3 나는 평일에 자주 빨래해요.

I __________ do the laundry on weekdays.

Day 18 Incidents & Accidents

Check Up Read and check the words you don't know.

1차 복습

- [ ] home
- [ ] dirty
- [ ] shower
- [ ] enjoy
- [ ] often
- [ ] automatic
- [ ] machine
- [ ] invent

2차 복습

- [ ] time
- [ ] year
- [ ] instead
- [ ] past

3차 복습

- [ ] weather
- [ ] holiday
- [ ] airport
- [ ] custom

※망각 제로! 1일 전 3일 전 7일 전 학습한 단어를 복습해요.

Word Tip

home 집	dirty 더러운	shower 샤워를 하다	enjoy 즐기다
often 자주, 흔히	automatic 자동의	machine 기계	invent 발명하다
time 시간	year 해, 년	instead 대신에	past 과거, 지나간
weather 날씨	holiday 휴일	airport 공항	custom 풍습, 관습

Rod is a superhero.

Pop Quiz Choose and check the right words.

The building is on fire.

건물에 ____________이 났어요.

☐ 불

☐ 기사

A hero saved the man in danger.

영웅이 위험에 빠진 사람을 ____________.

☐ 구하다

☐ 생각하다

Catch Up

Listen & Say

Listen, say, and color.

Read & Write

Write the **Basic Words** and **Jump Up Words.**

find
찾다, 발견하다

v

I need to find my key.

내 열쇠를 찾아야 해요.

save
구하다, 모으다

v

He saved the people in danger.

그는 위험에 처한 사람들을 구했어요.

hero
영웅

n

That brave firefighter is a hero.

저 용감한 소방관은 영웅이에요.

fire
불

n

The fire quickly spread.
불은 빠르게 번졌어요.

safe
안전한

a

This place is safe.
이 장소는 안전해요.

shout
소리치다

v

I shout loudly in the mountains.
나는 산에서 큰 소리로 외쳐요.

consider
생각하다, 여기다

v

We need to consider if it's safe.
우리는 그것이 안전한지 생각할 필요가 있어요.

article
기사, 글

n

There was an article on the plane accident.
비행기 사고에 대한 기사가 있었어요.

Skill UP

A Choose and write the words.

article　　shout　　save

1 

소리치다

2 

구하다, 모으다

3 

기사, 글

B Cross out, unscramble, and write the words.

1 불　i r f u e

2 영웅　l e h o r

3 생각하다, 여기다　o n i s c e r d a

4 안전한　s u f e a

C Connect and fill in the blanks.

1 

2 

3 

That brave firefighter is a hero.
저 용감한 소방관은 __________이에요.

I need to find my key.
내 열쇠를 __________야 해요.

The fire quickly spread.
__________은 빠르게 번졌어요.

D Rearrange and write the sentences.

1 이 장소는 안전해요.

is | This | safe | place | .

2 나는 산에서 큰 소리로 외쳐요.

I | in | shout loudly | the mountains | .

Day 19

Events

Check Up Read and check the words you don't know.

1차 복습

- [ ] find
- [ ] save
- [ ] hero
- [ ] fire
- [ ] safe
- [ ] shout
- [ ] consider
- [ ] article

2차 복습

- [ ] breakfast
- [ ] lunch
- [ ] approve
- [ ] perfect

3차 복습

- [ ] late
- [ ] always
- [ ] try
- [ ] recommend

※망각 제로! 1일 전 3일 전 7일 전 학습한 단어를 복습해요.

Word Tip

find 찾다, 발견하다
safe 안전한
breakfast 아침 식사
late 늦은, 늦게

save 구하다, 모으다
shout 소리치다
lunch 점심 식사
always 항상

hero 영웅
consider 생각하다, 여기다
approve 찬성하다
try 노력하다, 시도하다

fire 불
article 기사, 글
perfect 완벽한
recommend 추천하다

Our teacher is getting married.

Pop Quiz Choose and check the right words.

Tomorrow is their teacher's wedding day.

__________은 선생님의 결혼식 날이에요.

- ☐ 오늘
- ☐ 내일

They are going to practice a wedding song.

친구들은 축가 __________ 거예요.

- ☐ 연습하다
- ☐ 결혼하다

Catch Up

Listen & Say Listen, say, and color.

Read & Write Write the **Basic Words** and **Jump Up Words.**

yesterday
어제

n adv

I went to the party yesterday.

나는 어제 파티에 갔어요.

today
오늘

n adv

Today is my wedding day.

오늘은 나의 결혼식 날이에요.

tomorrow
내일

n adv

We are going on our honeymoon tomorrow.

우리는 내일 신혼여행을 가요.

practice
연습하다, 연습

v n

I practice the dance.

나는 춤을 연습해요.

marry
결혼하다

v

Will you marry me?

나와 결혼해 줄래요?

barrier
장애물, 장벽

n

Stairs were a barrier for some guests.

몇몇 손님들에게 계단은 장애물이었어요.

language
언어

n

Some guests spoke a different language.

몇몇 손님들은 다른 언어를 말했어요.

crush
홀딱 반함, 강렬한 사랑

n

I had a crush on her.

나는 그녀에게 완전히 반했어요.

Skill UP

A Choose and write the words.

marry	practice	crush

1 

연습하다, 연습

2 

결혼하다

3 

홀딱 반함, 강렬한 사랑

B Choose and write the words.

yesterday	language	today	barrier

1 언어

2 장애물, 장벽

3 오늘

4 어제

C Unscramble and complete the sentences.

❶ 

몇몇 손님들에게 계단은 장애물이었어요. **irbarre**

Stairs were a ______________ for some guests.

❷ 

몇몇 손님들은 다른 언어를 말했어요. **alngauge**

Some guests spoke a different ______________.

❸ 

오늘은 나의 결혼식 날이에요. **daoTy**

______________ is my wedding day.

D Choose and complete the sentences.

tomorrow	marry	practice

❶ 나와 결혼해 줄래요?

Will you ______________ me?

❷ 우리는 내일 신혼여행을 가요.

We are going on our honeymoon ______________.

❸ 나는 춤을 연습해요.

I ______________ the dance.

Day 20

Daily Routines

Check Up Read and check the words you don't know.

1차 복습

- [ ] yesterday
- [ ] today
- [ ] tomorrow
- [ ] practice
- [ ] marry
- [ ] barrier
- [ ] language
- [ ] crush

2차 복습

- [ ] home
- [ ] dirty
- [ ] machine
- [ ] invent

3차 복습

- [ ] wrong
- [ ] fight
- [ ] fix
- [ ] prove

※망각 제로! 1일 전 3일 전 7일 전 학습한 단어를 복습해요.

Word Tip

yesterday 어제
today 오늘
tomorrow 내일
practice 연습하다, 연습
marry 결혼하다
barrier 장애물, 장벽
language 언어
crush 홀딱 반함, 강렬한 사랑
home 집
dirty 더러운
machine 기계
invent 발명하다
wrong 잘못된, 틀린
fight 싸우다
fix 고치다
prove 증명하다

I can't wait to eat chicken.

Pop Quiz Choose and check the right words.

The chicken will take 1 hour to cook.

치킨은 요리하는 데 1시간이 ____________.

☐ (시간이) 걸리다

☐ 조사하다

Dennis hasn't finished his homework yet.

데니스는 숙제를 아직 ____________ 않았어요.

☐ 끝내다

☐ 알리다

Catch Up

Listen & Say Listen, say, and color.

Read & Write Write the **Basic Words** and **Jump Up Words.**

take
(시간이) 걸리다, 가지고 가다

v

It **takes** ten minutes to walk to school.

학교까지 걸어서 10분이 걸려요.

never
절대 ~ 않다

adv

I **never** forget to brush my teeth.

나는 이 닦는 것을 절대 잊지 않아요.

finish
끝내다

v

I **finish** my homework before dinner.

나는 저녁 식사 전에 숙제를 끝내요.

hour
시간

n

It takes me an hour to get ready.

나는 준비하는 데 한 시간이 걸려요.

minute
분

n

It is only a minute on foot.

걸어서 1분밖에 안 걸려요.

yet
아직

adv

I haven't finished my homework yet.

나는 아직 숙제를 끝내지 못했어요.

report
보고서,
알리다

n v

I'm working on a report for school.

나는 학교에 제출할 보고서를 작성하고 있어요.

research
조사, 연구,
조사하다

n v

I need to do some research.

내가 조사를 좀 해야겠어요.

Skill UP

A Choose and write the words.

hour minute report

❶ 

분

❷ 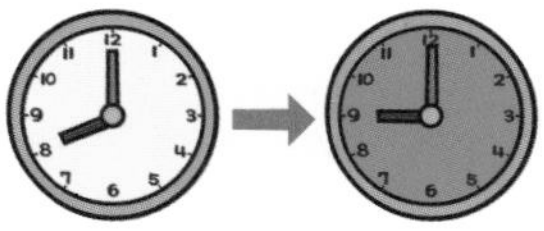

시간

❸ 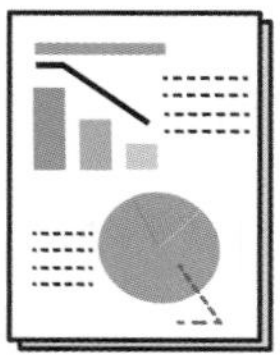

보고서, 알리다

B Cross out, unscramble, and write the words.

❶ (시간이) 걸리다, 가지고 가다 — a r t e k

❷ 끝내다 — i f n h s e i

❸ 아직 — y z e t

❹ 절대 ~ 않다 — e u v n e r

C Connect and fill in the blanks.

❶ 

❷ 

❸ 

I finish my homework before dinner.

나는 저녁 식사 전에 숙제를 ____________.

I need to do some research.

내가 ____________를 좀 해야겠어요.

It takes ten minutes to walk to school.

학교까지 걸어서 10분이 ____________.

D Rearrange and write the sentences.

❶ 걸어서 1분밖에 안 걸려요.

is | It | only a minute | foot | on | .

❷ 나는 이 닦는 것을 절대 잊지 않아요.

I | to | brush | never forget | teeth | my | .

WORD PUZZLE

Find and circle the pictures.
Then write the words.

Word Bank

집 ♥ 결혼하다
불 ♥ 샤워를 하다
기계 ♥ 기사
영웅 ♥ 보고서

article

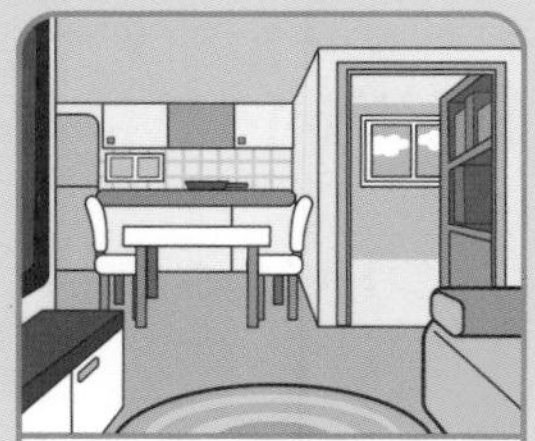

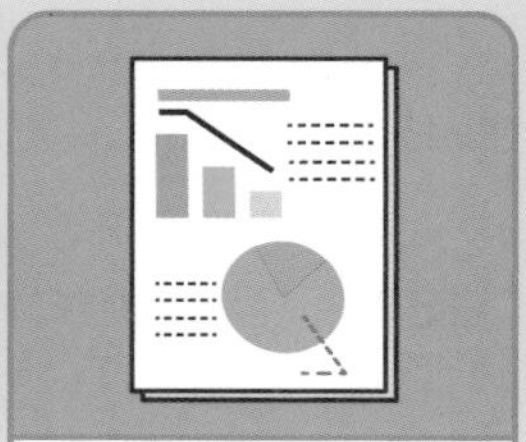

Day 16~20

breakfast 아침 식사	**lunch** 점심 식사	**dinner** 저녁 식사	**picnic** 소풍	**quick** 빠른

spot 장소	**approve** 찬성하다	**perfect** 완벽한	**home** 집	**dirty** 더러운
		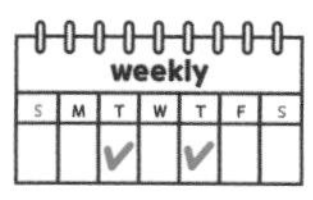		
shower 샤워를 하다	**enjoy** 즐기다	**often** 자주, 흔히	**automatic** 자동의	**machine** 기계

invent 발명하다	**find** 찾다, 발견하다	**save** 구하다, 모으다	**hero** 영웅	**fire** 불
				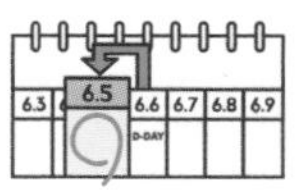
safe 안전한	**shout** 소리치다	**consider** 생각하다, 여기다	**article** 기사, 글	**yesterday** 어제
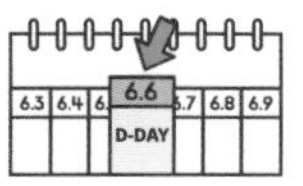	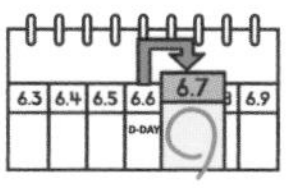			
today 오늘	**tomorrow** 내일	**practice** 연습하다, 연습	**marry** 결혼하다	**barrier** 장애물, 장벽

language 언어	**crush** 홀딱 반함, 강렬한 사랑	**take** (시간이) 걸리다, 가지고 가다	**never** 절대 ~ 않다	**finish** 끝내다
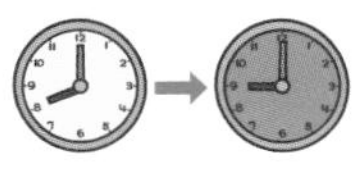			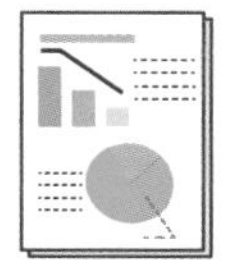	
hour 시간	**minute** 분	**yet** 아직	**report** 보고서, 알리다	**research** 조사, 연구, 조사하다

Review TEST

맞힌 개수 : ☐ / 40

① breakfast		㉑ 빠른	
② lunch		㉒ 장소	
③ dinner		㉓ 찬성하다	
④ picnic		㉔ 완벽한	
⑤ home		㉕ 자주, 흔히	
⑥ dirty		㉖ 자동의	
⑦ shower		㉗ 기계	
⑧ enjoy		㉘ 발명하다	
⑨ find		㉙ 안전한	
⑩ save		㉚ 소리치다	
⑪ hero		㉛ 생각하다, 여기다	
⑫ fire		㉜ 기사, 글	
⑬ yesterday		㉝ 결혼하다	
⑭ today		㉞ 장애물, 장벽	
⑮ tomorrow		㉟ 언어	
⑯ crush		㊱ 연습하다, 연습	
⑰ take		㊲ 분	
⑱ never		㊳ 아직	
⑲ finish		㊴ 보고서, 알리다	
⑳ research		㊵ 시간	

Part 5

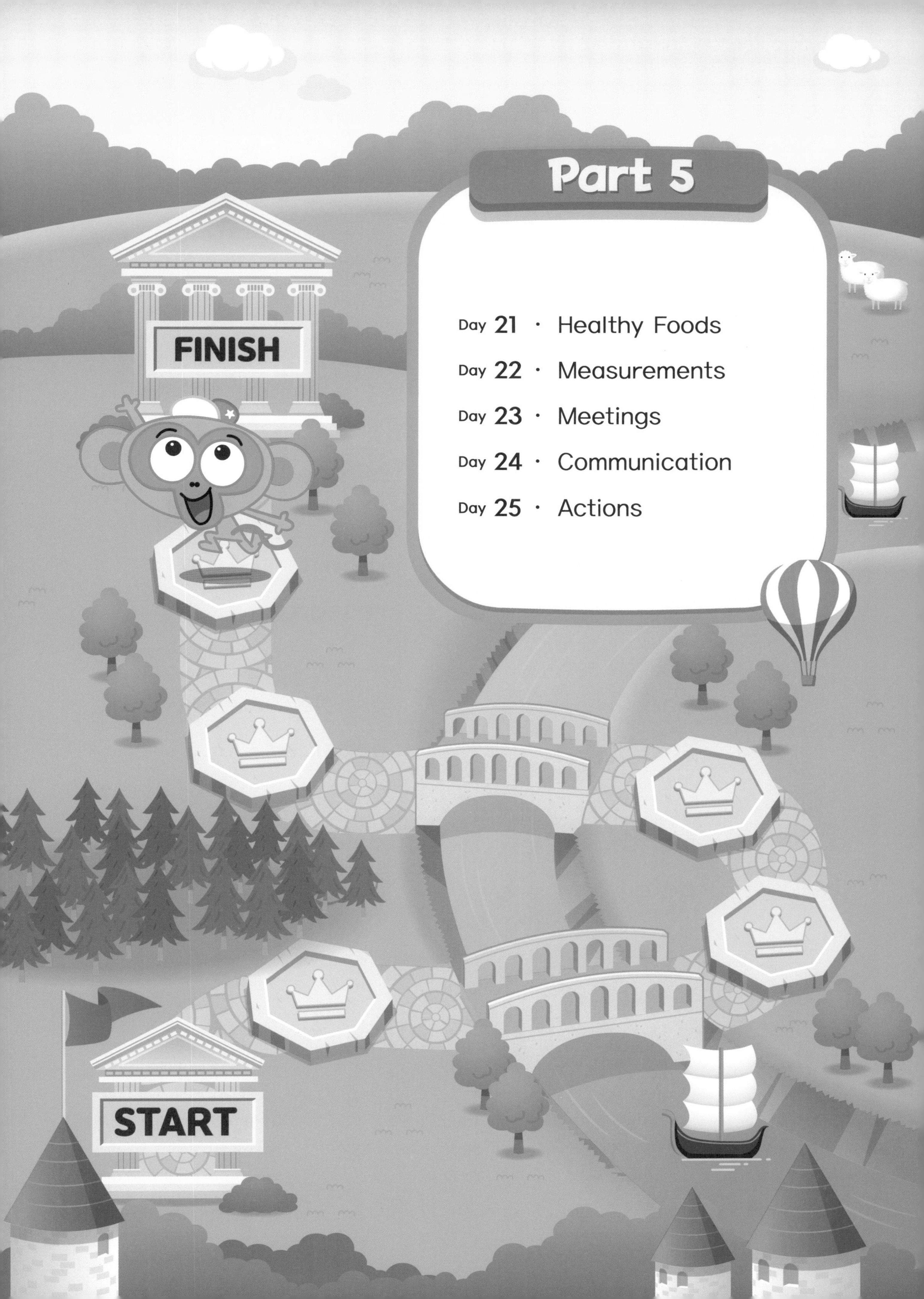

Day 21

Healthy Foods

Check Up Read and check the words you don't know.

1차 복습

- [ ] hour
- [ ] never
- [ ] finish
- [ ] take
- [ ] minute
- [ ] yet
- [ ] report
- [ ] research

2차 복습

- [ ] find
- [ ] save
- [ ] article
- [ ] consider

3차 복습

- [ ] month
- [ ] date
- [ ] day
- [ ] brief

※망각 제로! 1일 전 3일 전 7일 전 학습한 단어를 복습해요.

Word Tip

hour 시간
minute 분
find 찾다, 발견하다
month 달, 월
never 절대 ~ 않다
yet 아직
save 구하다, 모으다
date 날짜
finish 끝내다
report 보고서, 알리다
article 기사, 글
day 하루, 날, 요일
take (시간이) 걸리다, 가지고 가다
research 조사, 연구, 조사하다
consider 생각하다, 여기다
brief 짧은, 간단한

Let's have a healthy breakfast.

Pop Quiz Choose and check the right words.

They should pick the blueberries that have turned a deep purple.

블루베리는 진한 보라색으로 ____________ 것만 따야 해요.

☐ 변하다

☐ 따다

The lettuce is very fresh.

상추가 아주 ____________요.

☐ 단단한

☐ 신선한

Catch UP

Listen & Say Listen, say, and color.

Read & Write Write the **Basic Words** and **Jump Up Words.**

pick
따다, 고르다

v

We picked fresh fruit.
우리는 신선한 과일을 땄어요.

fruit
과일

n

My family likes to eat fruit.
우리 가족은 과일 먹는 것을 좋아해요.

vegetable
채소

n

You should eat vegetables.
당신은 채소를 먹어야 해요.

turn

차례, 돌다, 변하다

It's your turn to make a sandwich. n v

당신이 샌드위치를 만들 차례예요.

fresh

신선한

Fresh food is good for your health. a

신선한 음식은 당신의 건강에 좋아요.

firm

단단한, 확고한

Make sure to choose firm fruits. a

단단한 과일을 선택하세요.

bunch

다발, 묶음

I bought a bunch of bananas. n

나는 바나나 한 다발을 샀어요.

raw

날것의, 익히지 않은

Eating raw vegetables is good. a

생채소를 먹는 것은 좋아요.

Skill UP

A Find, circle, and write the words.

1. 

   gmpickme

   따다, 고르다

2. 

   sfruitowz

   과일

3. 

   aiturnta

   차례, 돌다, 변하다

4. 

   vxhfirmc

   단단한, 확고한

B Choose and write the words.

vegetable fresh raw bunch

1. 채소
2. 날것의, 익히지 않은
3. 다발, 묶음
4. 신선한

C Unscramble and complete the sentences.

1 

신선한 음식은 당신의 건강에 좋아요.

e r F s h

_______ food is good for your health.

2 

나는 바나나 한 다발을 샀어요.

u b n h c

I bought a _______ of bananas.

3 

생채소를 먹는 것은 좋아요.

w a r

Eating _______ vegetables is good.

D Rearrange and write the sentences.

1 우리는 신선한 과일을 땄어요.

We | fresh | picked | fruit | .

2 단단한 과일을 선택하세요.

sure | Make | fruits | choose | firm | to | .

Day 22

Measurements

Check Up Read and check the words you don't know.

1차 복습

- [ ] pick
- [ ] fruit
- [ ] vegetable
- [ ] turn
- [ ] fresh
- [ ] firm
- [ ] bunch
- [ ] raw

2차 복습

- [ ] yesterday
- [ ] today
- [ ] language
- [ ] crush

3차 복습

- [ ] dinner
- [ ] picnic
- [ ] quick
- [ ] spot

※**망각 제로!** 1일 전 3일 전 7일 전 학습한 단어를 복습해요.

Word Tip

pick 따다, 고르다
fresh 신선한
yesterday 어제
dinner 저녁 식사

fruit 과일
firm 단단한, 확고한
today 오늘
picnic 소풍

vegetable 채소
bunch 다발, 묶음
language 언어
quick 빠른

turn 차례, 돌다, 변하다
raw 날것의, 익히지 않은
crush 홀딱 반함, 강렬한 사랑
spot 장소

This one is very heavy.

Pop Quiz Choose and check the right words.

The weights of the kettle bells vary from size to size.

케틀벨의 무게는 크기에 따라 ____________.

☐ 서로 다르다

☐ 가벼운

Dennis tries to lift one.

데니스는 케틀벨을 ____________려고 시도해요.

☐ 들어 올리다

☐ 무거운

Catch Up

Listen & Say Listen, say, and color.

Read & Write Write the **Basic Words** and **Jump Up Words.**

weight
무게

n

I don't know the weight.

나는 무게를 몰라요.

heavy
무거운

a

The rock is heavy.

바위는 무거워요.

light
가벼운, 밝은

a

The feather is light.

깃털은 가벼워요.

watermelon
수박

ⓝ

This **watermelon** weighs 5 kg.

이 **수박**의 무게는 5 kg이에요.

size
크기

ⓝ

The **size** of the box is small.

그 상자의 **크기**는 작아요.

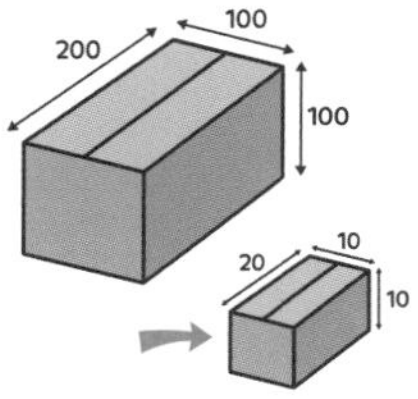

force
힘, 폭력

ⓝ

They did a science experiment on **force**.

그들은 **힘**에 대한 과학 실험을 했어요.

vary
서로 다르다, 달라지다

ⓥ

The lengths of rulers can **vary**.

자의 길이는 **서로 다를** 수 있어요.

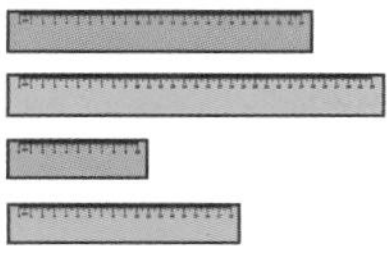

lift
들어 올리다

ⓥ

I had to **lift** a heavy suitcase.

나는 무거운 여행 가방을 **들어 올려**야 했어요.

Skill UP

A Choose and write the words.

size force weight

❶ 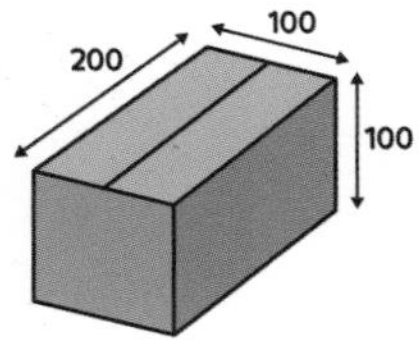

크기

❷ 

무게

❸ 

힘, 폭력

B Cross out, unscramble, and write the words.

❶ 무거운 y x h e v a

❷ 가벼운, 밝은 l u g h i t

❸ 들어 올리다 l f t g i

❹ 서로 다르다, 달라지다 a v r y e

C Connect and fill in the blanks.

1 

2 

3 

The feather is light.
깃털은 ______________ 요.

The rock is heavy.
바위는 ______________ 요.

This watermelon weighs 5 kg.
이 ______________ 의 무게는 5 kg이에요.

D Rearrange and write the sentences.

1 나는 무거운 여행 가방을 들어 올려야 했어요.

lift | I | had to | suitcase | a heavy | .

2 자의 길이는 서로 다를 수 있어요.

of rulers | The lengths | can | vary | .

Day 23 Meetings

Check Up Read and check the words you don't know.

1차 복습

- [ ] weight
- [ ] heavy
- [ ] light
- [ ] watermelon
- [ ] size
- [ ] force
- [ ] vary
- [ ] lift

2차 복습

- [ ] take
- [ ] never
- [ ] report
- [ ] research

3차 복습

- [ ] shower
- [ ] enjoy
- [ ] automatic
- [ ] often

※**망각 제로!** 1일 전 3일 전 7일 전 학습한 단어를 복습해요.

Word Tip

weight 무게	**heavy** 무거운	**light** 가벼운, 밝은	**watermelon** 수박
size 크기	**force** 힘, 폭력	**vary** 서로 다르다, 달라지다	**lift** 들어 올리다
take (시간이) 걸리다, 가지고 가다	**never** 절대 ~ 않다	**report** 보고서, 알리다	**research** 조사, 연구, 조사하다
shower 샤워를 하다	**enjoy** 즐기다	**automatic** 자동의	**often** 자주, 흔히

Today is an important day.

Pop Quiz Choose and check the right words.

Today is an important day.

오늘은 ______________ 날이에요.

☐ 어두운

☐ 중요한

Kiara and Sally will leave early next time.

키아라와 샐리는 ______________에 일찍 출발할 거예요.

☐ 다음의

☐ 건너다

Catch UP

Listen & Say Listen, say, and color.

Read & Write Write the Basic Words and Jump Up Words.

cross 건너다 (v)

Let's cross the road.

길을 건너가자.

important 중요한 (a)

It is important to listen to others.

다른 사람의 말을 듣는 것은 중요해요.

dark 어두운 (a)

I can't see anything in the dark.

나는 어둠 속에서 아무것도 볼 수 없어요.

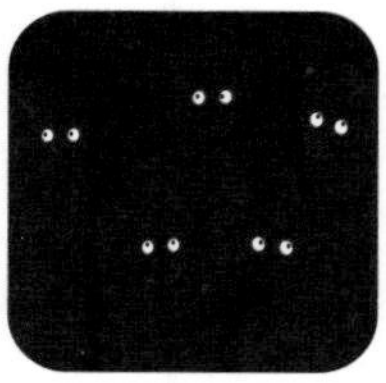

change
바꾸다, 변화

v n

We need to **change** our goal.
우리는 목표를 **바꿔**야 해요.

next
다음의,
그 다음에

a adv

Our meeting is **next** Tuesday.
우리의 회의는 **다음** 주 화요일이에요.

traffic
차량들, 교통

n

I'm stuck in **traffic**.
교통체증 때문에 꼼짝 못 해요.

pool
수영장, 웅덩이

n

Let's meet at the **pool**.
수영장에서 만나자.

prepare
준비하다

v

I will **prepare** for the meeting.
나는 회의를 **준비할게요**.

Skill UP

A Choose and write the words.

dark pool change

1 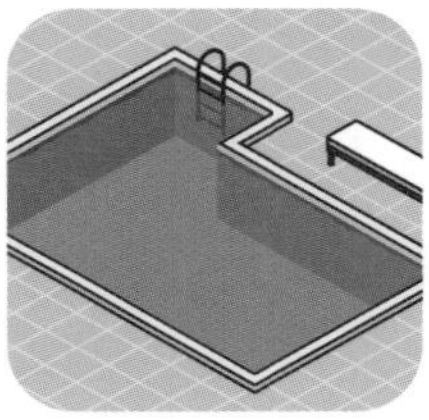

수영장, 웅덩이

2 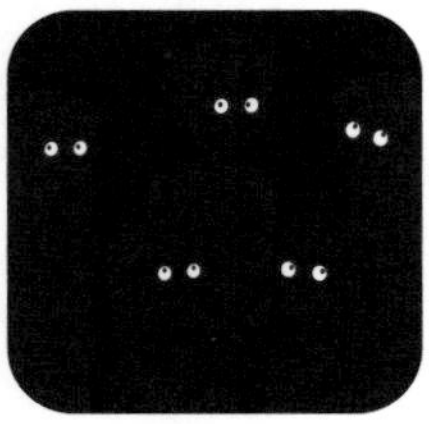

어두운

3 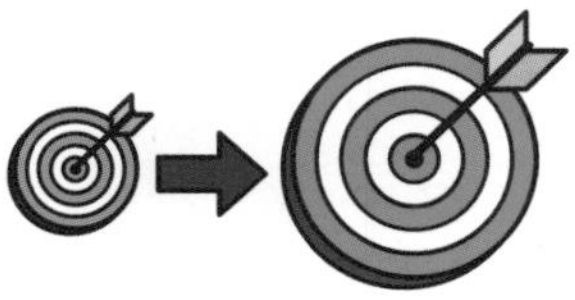

바꾸다, 변화

B Choose and write the words.

next important prepare traffic

1 차량들, 교통

2 준비하다

3 다음의, 그 다음에

4 중요한

C Unscramble and complete the sentences.

❶ 

길을 건너가자.

orcss

Let's ____________ the road.

❷ 

교통체증 때문에 꼼짝 못 해요.

raticff

I'm stuck in ____________.

❸ 

나는 회의를 준비할게요.

reppaer

I will ____________ for the meeting.

D Choose and complete the sentences.

important　　next　　change

❶ 다른 사람의 말을 듣는 것은 중요해요.

It is ____________ to listen to others.

❷ 우리는 목표를 바꿔야 해요.

We need to ____________ our goal.

❸ 우리의 회의는 다음 주 화요일이에요.

Our meeting is ____________ Tuesday.

Day 24 Communication

Check Up Read and check the words you don't know.

1차 복습

- [ ] cross
- [ ] important
- [ ] dark
- [ ] change
- [ ] next
- [ ] traffic
- [ ] pool
- [ ] prepare

2차 복습

- [ ] pick
- [ ] fruit
- [ ] bunch
- [ ] raw

3차 복습

- [ ] hero
- [ ] fire
- [ ] safe
- [ ] shout

※망각 제로! 1일 전 3일 전 7일 전 학습한 단어를 복습해요.

Word Tip

cross 건너다
next 다음의, 그 다음에
pick 따다, 고르다
hero 영웅
important 중요한
traffic 차량들, 교통
fruit 과일
fire 불
dark 어두운
pool 수영장, 웅덩이
bunch 다발, 묶음
safe 안전한
change 바꾸다, 변화
prepare 준비하다
raw 날것의, 익히지 않은
shout 소리치다

We can't focus on the class.

Pop Quiz Choose and check the right words.

Everyone is focusing on the class.

모두 ____________에 집중하고 있어요.

☐ 수업
☐ 교과서

A bee is interrupting the class.

벌이 수업을 ____________ 있어요.

☐ 방해하다
☐ 집중하다

Catch Up

Listen & Say Listen, say, and color.

Read & Write Write the Basic Words and Jump Up Words.

focus
집중하다, 초점

v n

You should focus on your work.
당신은 당신의 일에 집중해야 해요.

lesson
수업

n

I will review the lesson.
나는 수업을 복습할 거예요.

quiet
조용한

a

Please be quiet in the library.
도서관에서는 조용히 해 주세요.

textbook
교과서

ⓝ

He borrows a textbook.
그는 교과서를 빌려요.

begin
시작하다

ⓥ

Let's begin the meeting.
회의를 시작하자.

manner
태도, 방식, 예의

ⓝ

Please talk in a respectful manner.
정중한 태도로 이야기해 주세요.

interrupt
방해하다,
중단시키다

ⓥ

Please do not interrupt others.
다른 사람을 방해하지 말아 주세요.

respect
존중, 존경하다

ⓝ ⓥ

We need to show respect.
우리는 존중을 보여줘야 해요.

Skill UP

A Find, circle, and write the words.

1 
수업

o l e s s o n v

2 
집중하다, 초점

t l r u f o c u s

3 
조용한

a q u i e t a d

4 
존중, 존경하다

v r e s p e c t

B Choose and write the words.

begin interrupt textbook manner

1 태도, 방식, 예의

2 방해하다, 중단시키다

3 교과서

4 시작하다

C Connect and fill in the blanks.

1 

• • Please do not interrupt others.

다른 사람을 ____________ 말아 주세요.

2 

• • Please talk in a respectful manner.

정중한 ____________로 이야기해 주세요.

3 

• • He borrows a textbook.

그는 ____________를 빌려요.

D Rearrange and write the sentences.

1 회의를 시작하자.

begin | Let's | the meeting | .

2 도서관에서는 조용히 해 주세요.

Please | quiet | the library | be | in | .

Day 25

Actions

Check Up Read and check the words you don't know.

1차 복습

- ☐ focus
- ☐ lesson
- ☐ quiet
- ☐ textbook
- ☐ begin
- ☐ manner
- ☐ interrupt
- ☐ respect

2차 복습

- ☐ weight
- ☐ heavy
- ☐ vary
- ☐ lift

3차 복습

- ☐ tomorrow
- ☐ practice
- ☐ marry
- ☐ barrier

※**망각 제로!** 1일 전 3일 전 7일 전 학습한 단어를 복습해요.

Word Tip

focus 집중하다, 초점	**lesson** 수업	**quiet** 조용한	**textbook** 교과서
begin 시작하다	**manner** 태도, 방식, 예의	**interrupt** 방해하다, 중단시키다	**respect** 존중, 존경하다
weight 무게	**heavy** 무거운	**vary** 서로 다르다, 달라지다	**lift** 들어 올리다
tomorrow 내일	**practice** 연습하다, 연습	**marry** 결혼하다	**barrier** 장애물, 장벽

Let's build a sandcastle!

Pop Quiz Choose and check the right words.

Rod and his friends are building a sandcastle.

친구들은 모래성을 ______ 있어요.

☐ 짓다

☐ 들어 올리다

Sally is going to put a flag on the top.

샐리는 ______을 꼭대기에 꽂을 거예요.

☐ 깃발

☐ 생각

Catch UP

Listen & Say Listen, say, and color.

Read & Write Write the **Basic Words** and **Jump Up Words.**

build
짓다

ⓥ They **build** a sandcastle.
그들은 모래성을 지어요.

flag
기, 깃발

ⓝ The **flag** waves in the wind.
깃발이 바람에 흔들려요.

top
꼭대기, 맨 위

ⓝ He climbs to the **top** of the mountain.
그가 산꼭대기에 올라요.

triangle
삼각형

n

I draw a triangle in my sketchbook.
나는 스케치북에 삼각형을 그려요.

idea
생각

n

What a good idea!
정말 좋은 생각이에요!

height
키, 높이

n

We measured our heights.
우리는 키를 쟀어요.

decorate
장식하다

v

We decorated the house.
우리는 집을 장식했어요.

approach
다가오다

v

We heard him approach.
우리는 그가 다가오는 소리를 들었어요.

Skill UP

A Choose and write the words.

build   decorate   approach

1 

짓다

2 

다가오다

3 

장식하다

B Choose and write the words.

triangle   height   flag   idea

1 기, 깃발

2 삼각형

3 생각

4 키, 높이

C Connect and fill in the blanks.

1 

2 

3 

I draw a triangle in my sketchbook.

나는 스케치북에 ________을 그려요.

He climbs to the top of the mountain.

그는 산 ________에 올라요.

What a good idea!

정말 좋은 ________이에요!

D Rearrange and write the sentences.

1 깃발이 바람에 흔들려요.

waves | The flag | the wind | in | .

2 우리는 키를 쟀어요.

We | our | measured | heights | .

WORD PUZZLE Complete the word puzzle.

ACROSS

② The rock is ________ .

④ I bought a ________ of bananas.

⑧ Let's meet at the ________ .

⑨ What a good ________ !

⑩ We need to show ________ .

DOWN

① Let's ________ the meeting.

③ He climbs to the ________ of the mountain.

⑤ Let's ________ the road.

⑥ I had to ________ a heavy suitcase.

⑦ Eating ________ vegetables is good.

pick 따다, 고르다	**fruit** 과일	**vegetable** 채소	**turn** 차례, 돌다, 변하다	**fresh** 신선한

firm 단단한, 확고한	**bunch** 다발, 묶음	**raw** 날것의, 익히지 않은	**weight** 무게	**heavy** 무거운
		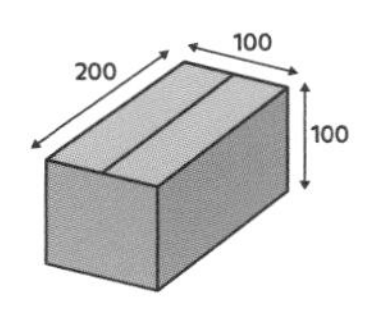		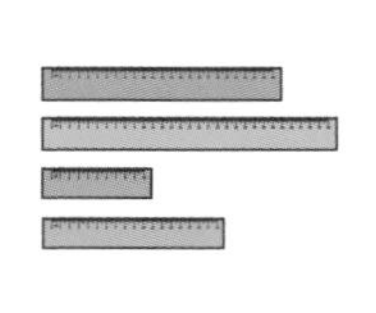
light 가벼운, 밝은	**watermelon** 수박	**size** 크기	**force** 힘, 폭력	**vary** 서로 다르다, 달라지다
				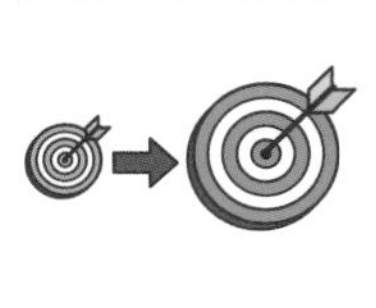
lift 들어 올리다	**cross** 건너다	**important** 중요한	**dark** 어두운	**change** 바꾸다, 변화

next 다음의, 그 다음에	**traffic** 차량들, 교통	**pool** 수영장, 웅덩이	**prepare** 준비하다	**focus** 집중하다, 초점

lesson 수업	**quiet** 조용한	**textbook** 교과서	**begin** 시작하다	**manner** 태도, 방식, 예의

interrupt 방해하다, 중단시키다	**respect** 존중, 존경하다	**build** 짓다	**flag** 기, 깃발	**top** 꼭대기, 맨 위

triangle 삼각형	**idea** 생각	**height** 키, 높이	**decorate** 장식하다	**approach** 다가오다

Day 21~25

Review TEST

맞힌 개수 : ☐ / 40

① raw		㉑ 신선한	
② fruit		㉒ 단단한, 확고한	
③ vegetable		㉓ 다발, 묶음	
④ turn		㉔ 따다, 고르다	
⑤ weight		㉕ 크기	
⑥ heavy		㉖ 힘, 폭력	
⑦ light		㉗ 수박	
⑧ vary		㉘ 들어 올리다	
⑨ next		㉙ 건너다	
⑩ important		㉚ 차량들, 교통	
⑪ dark		㉛ 수영장, 웅덩이	
⑫ change		㉜ 준비하다	
⑬ focus		㉝ 시작하다	
⑭ lesson		㉞ 태도, 방식, 예의	
⑮ interrupt		㉟ 조용한	
⑯ textbook		㊱ 존중, 존경하다	
⑰ build		㊲ 생각	
⑱ flag		㊳ 키, 높이	
⑲ top		㊴ 장식하다	
⑳ triangle		㊵ 다가오다	

Answer Key

Level 2.2

Day 01

P11

Pop Quiz ☐ 목표 ☑ 물건 ☑ 밴드 ☐ 조깅

P14~15

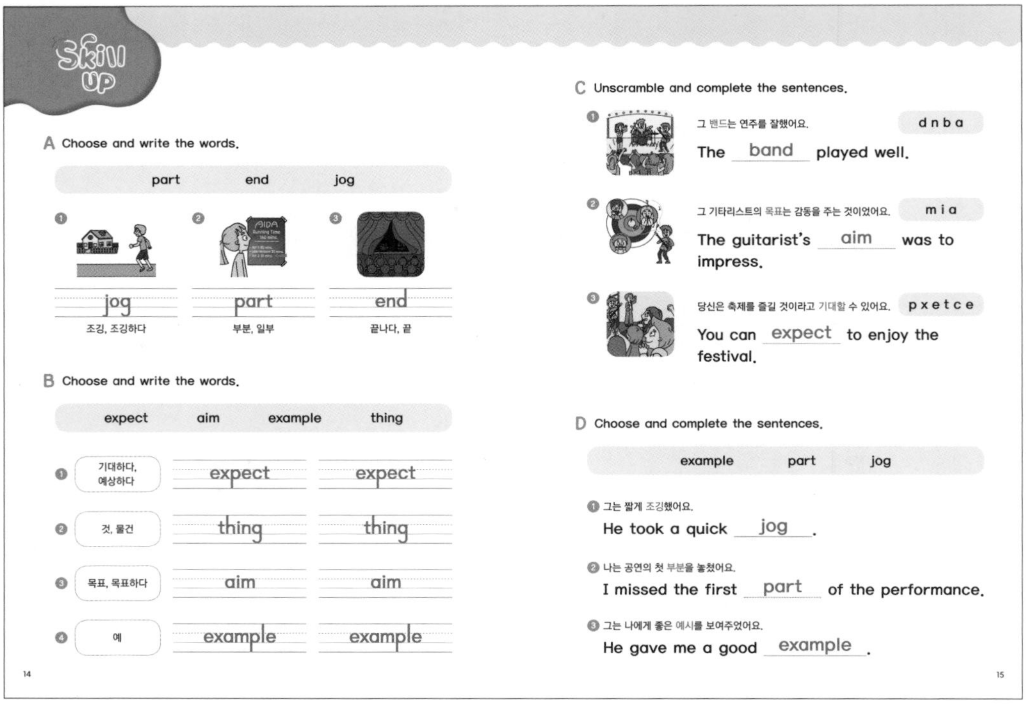
Skill Up

A Choose and write the words.

part end jog

❶ jog 조깅, 조깅하다
❷ part 부분, 일부
❸ end 끝나다, 끝

B Choose and write the words.

expect aim example thing

❶ 기대하다, 예상하다	expect	expect
❷ 것, 물건	thing	thing
❸ 목표, 목표하다	aim	aim
❹ 예	example	example

C Unscramble and complete the sentences.

❶ 그 밴드는 연주를 잘했어요. dnba
The band played well.

❷ 그 기타리스트의 목표는 감동을 주는 것이었어요. mia
The guitarist's aim was to impress.

❸ 당신은 축제를 즐길 것이라고 기대할 수 있어요. pxetce
You can expect to enjoy the festival.

D Choose and complete the sentences.

example part jog

❶ 그는 짧게 조깅했어요.
He took a quick jog.

❷ 나는 공연의 첫 부분을 놓쳤어요.
I missed the first part of the performance.

❸ 그는 나에게 좋은 예시를 보여주었어요.
He gave me a good example.

14 15

Day 02

P17

Pop Quiz ☑ 감기 ☐ 열 ☑ 두통 ☐ 건강

P20~21

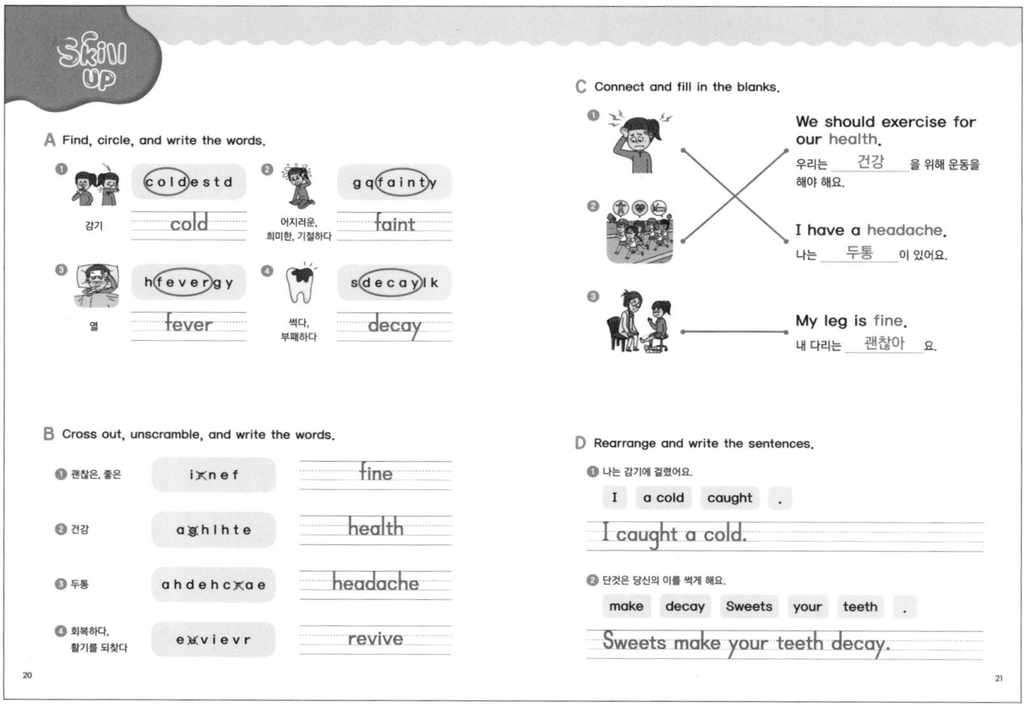
Skill Up

A Find, circle, and write the words.

❶ coldestd — cold 감기
❷ gqfainty — faint 어지러운, 희미한, 기절하다
❸ hfeverqy — fever 열
❹ sdecaylk — decay 썩다, 부패하다

B Cross out, unscramble, and write the words.

❶ 괜찮은, 좋은 — ixnef — fine
❷ 건강 — agxhlhte — health
❸ 두통 — ahdehcxae — headache
❹ 회복하다, 활기를 되찾다 — exvievr — revive

C Connect and fill in the blanks.

❶ — I have a headache. 나는 두통이 있어요.
❷ — We should exercise for our health. 우리는 건강을 위해 운동을 해야 해요.
❸ — My leg is fine. 내 다리는 괜찮아요.

D Rearrange and write the sentences.

❶ 나는 감기에 걸렸어요.
I / a cold / caught / .
I caught a cold.

❷ 단것은 당신의 이를 썩게 해요.
make / decay / Sweets / your / teeth / .
Sweets make your teeth decay.

20 21

Day 03

P23

Pop Quiz ☐ 편지 ☑ 잔디 ☐ 적절한 ☑ 미안한

P26~27

Skill Up

A Choose and write the words.

lawn sorry guide

❶ 
lawn
잔디

❷ 
guide
안내하다, 이끌다

❸ 
sorry
미안한, 안쓰러운

B Choose and write the words.

express thank proper again

❶ 감사하다, 고마워하다	thank	thank
❷ 적절한, 올바른	proper	proper
❸ 다시, 한 번 더	again	again
❹ 표현하다, 나타내다	express	express

26

C Unscramble and complete the sentences.

❶ 
나는 우리 선생님께 감사드려요. hantk
I thank my teacher.

❷ 
나는 할머니께 편지를 썼어요. tletre
I wrote a letter to my grandma.

❸ 
적절한 예의범절을 사용하는 것이 중요해요. poprre
It's important to use proper manners.

D Choose and complete the sentences.

lawn guide express

❶ 나를 안내해 줄 수 있나요?
Can you guide me?

❷ 잔디 위에서 캐치볼을 하자.
Let's play catch on the lawn.

❸ 나는 내 감정을 표현하는 것을 좋아해요.
I like to express my feelings.

27

Day 04

P29

Pop Quiz ☑ 스트레스 ☐ 시험 ☐ 어깨 ☑ 결과

P32~33

Skill Up

A Choose and write the words.

test struggle learn

❶ 
learn
배우다

❷ 
test
시험

❸ 
struggle
힘겹게 하다, 허우적거리다

B Cross out, unscramble, and write the words.

❶ 결과	e r l u ~~x~~ s t	result
❷ 반, 수업	l a s c s ~~x~~	class
❸ 어깨	o h s u d ~~x~~ l r e	shoulder
❹ 스트레스, 압박	s ~~x~~ t e s r s	stress

32

C Connect and fill in the blanks.

❶ 
❷ 
❸ 

I got a good result.
나는 좋은 결과 를 얻었어요.

I put my backpack on my shoulder.
나는 배낭을 어깨 에 멨어요.

We have an art class today.
우리는 오늘 미술 수업 이 있어요.

D Rearrange and write the sentences.

❶ 나는 숙제를 해요.
do my I homework .
I do my homework.

❷ 너무 많은 숙제는 스트레스의 원인이 돼요.
stress Too much causes homework .
Too much homework causes stress.

33

Day 05

P35

Pop Quiz ☑ 둘 다(의) ☐ 연약한 ☑ ~을 더 좋아하다 ☐ 회복하다

P38~39

Skill Up

A Find, circle, and write the words.

1. 소고기 — a m c (b e e f) y — beef
2. 돼지고기 — q w b (p o r k) m — pork
3. 계산서 — u b m r t (b i l l) — bill
4. 비용, 값 — z n (c o s t) e z — cost

B Choose and write the words.

delicate advantage prefer both

1. 둘 다(의) — both — both
2. ~을 더 좋아하다 — prefer — prefer
3. 연약한, 섬세한 — delicate — delicate
4. 장점, 이점 — advantage — advantage

38

C Connect and fill in the blanks.

1. I bought both milk and yogurt.
나는 우유와 요구르트를 둘 다 샀어요.
2. I prefer to buy fresh food.
나는 신선한 음식을 사는 것 을 더 좋아해요.
3. This cup looks very delicate.
이 컵은 매우 연약해 보여요.

D Choose and complete the sentences.

bills cost beef

1. 소고기 좀 사는 게 어때요?
How about buying some beef ?
2. 나는 항상 계산서를 확인해요.
I always check the bills .
3. 영수증에는 총비용이 나와 있어요.
The receipt shows the total cost .

39

Day 01~05

P40

P42

Review TEST

맞힌 개수 : ☐ / 40

1 part	부분, 일부	21 끝나다, 끝	end
2 example	예	22 목표, 목표하다	aim
3 thing	것, 물건	23 조깅, 조깅하다	jog
4 expect	기대하다, 예상하다	24 밴드, 그룹	band
5 cold	감기	25 두통	headache
6 faint	어지러운, 희미한, 기절하다	26 열	fever
7 revive	회복하다, 활기를 되찾다	27 건강	health
8 fine	괜찮은, 좋은	28 썩다, 부패하다	decay
9 thank	감사하다, 고마워하다	29 편지	letter
10 sorry	미안한, 안쓰러운	30 적절한, 올바른	proper
11 express	표현하다, 나타내다	31 다시, 한 번 더	again
12 guide	안내하다, 이끌다	32 잔디	lawn
13 stress	스트레스, 압박	33 반, 수업	class
14 struggle	힘겹게 하다, 허우적거리다	34 배우다	learn
15 homework	숙제	35 결과	result
16 test	시험	36 어깨	shoulder
17 pork	돼지고기	37 비용, 값	cost
18 beef	소고기	38 ~을 더 좋아하다	prefer
19 bill	계산서	39 연약한, 섬세한	delicate
20 both	둘 다(의)	40 장점, 이점	advantage

42

Day 06

P45

Pop Quiz

- [x] 세계
- [ ] 국가
- [x] 소도시
- [ ] 장소

P48~49

Skill Up

A Choose and write the words.

town country distant

1.  town — 소도시, 시내
2.  distant — 먼, 동떨어진
3.  country — 국가, 나라

B Choose and write the words.

rapid world place abundant

1. 세계	world	world
2. 풍부한	abundant	abundant
3. 빠른	rapid	rapid
4. 장소, 곳	place	place

C Unscramble and complete the sentences.

1.  나는 전 세계를 여행하고 싶어요. (owrld)
   I want to travel all over the world.
2.  나는 도시에 살아요. (cyti)
   I live in the city.
3.  그 강은 빠른 속도로 흘러갔어요. (rdapi)
   The river flowed at a rapid pace.

D Rearrange and write the sentences.

1. 어느 나라에서 오셨어요?
   you / from / What / country / are / ?
   What country are you from?
2. 나무가 많이 있어요.
   There / trees / are / abundant / .
   There are abundant trees.

Day 07

P51

Pop Quiz

- [ ] 머무르다
- [x] 청소하다
- [ ] 먼지
- [x] 세탁

P54~55

Skill Up

A Find, circle, and write the words.

1.  chwaitlp — wait (기다리다)
2.  kgdustim — dust (먼지)
3.  efcleanf — clean (청소하다)
4.  rlaundry — laundry (세탁, 세탁물)

B Cross out, unscramble, and write the words.

1. 재활용하다	eecxylrc	recycle
2. 주말	keenedxw	weekend
3. 머무르다	ayxst	stay
4. 씻다	hxswa	wash

C Connect and fill in the blanks.

1. 
2. 
3. 

- I help my mom on weekends. 나는 주말 마다 엄마를 도와요.
- I wash my hands. 나는 내 손을 씻어요.
- I recycle paper, plastic, and cans. 나는 종이, 플라스틱, 캔을 재활용해요.

D Choose and complete the sentences.

laundry stay dust

1. 나는 집에 머물러요.
   I stay at home.
2. 나는 선반의 먼지를 닦아요.
   I wipe the dust off the bookshelf.
3. 나는 세탁을 하고 있어요.
   I am doing the laundry.

Day 08

P57

Pop Quiz ☑ 잘생긴 ☐ 재미있는 ☑ 정직한 ☐ 우아한

P60~61

Skill Up

A Choose and write the words.

handsome fun grace

❶  grace 우아함, 품위

❷  fun 재미있는

❸  handsome 잘생긴, 멋진

B Choose and write the words.

rare honest legend famous

❶ 정직한	honest	honest
❷ 전설적인 인물, 전설	legend	legend
❸ 유명한	famous	famous
❹ 드문, 희귀한	rare	rare

60

C Unscramble and complete the sentences.

❶  우리 아빠는 훌륭한 요리사예요. r e a g t
My dad is a great cook.

❷  그 가수는 유명해요. a u f o m s
The singer is famous.

❸  정직해지는 것은 중요해요. h e o s t n
It's important to be honest.

D Rearrange and write the sentences.

❶ 수영장에서 수영하는 것은 재미있어요.
in / Swimming / fun / the pool / is / .
Swimming in the pool is fun.

❷ 우리 할아버지는 전설적인 분이셨어요.
My / a legend / was / grandpa / .
My grandpa is a legend.

61

Day 09

P63

Pop Quiz ☑ 치과 의사 ☐ 경찰 ☐ 가치 ☑ 꿈

P66~67

Skill Up

A Choose and write the words.

work arrest grow

❶  work 일하다, 일

❷  grow 재배하다, 자라다

❸  arrest 체포하다

B Cross out, unscramble, and write the words.

❶ 꿈, 꿈꾸다	d a e r x m	dream
❷ 치과 의사	t e n d s t x i	dentist
❸ 가치	a x v u e l	value
❹ 투자하다	e s i v t x n	invest

66

C Connect and fill in the blanks.

❶ 

❷ 

❸ 

My dad is a dentist.
우리 아빠는 치과 의사 예요.

Someone call the police!
누가 경찰 을 불러 주세요!

My dream is to be an artist.
나의 꿈 은 예술가예요.

D Choose and complete the sentences.

invest work value

❶ 그는 8시에 일하러 가요.
He goes to work at 8.

❷ 나의 부모님은 돈 투자를 잘하세요.
My parents invest money well.

❸ 팀워크는 나에게 중요한 가치예요.
Teamwork is an important value to me.

67

Day 10

P69

Pop Quiz ☐ 예측하다 ☑ 맞이하다 ☑ 이야기 ☐ 질문

P72~73

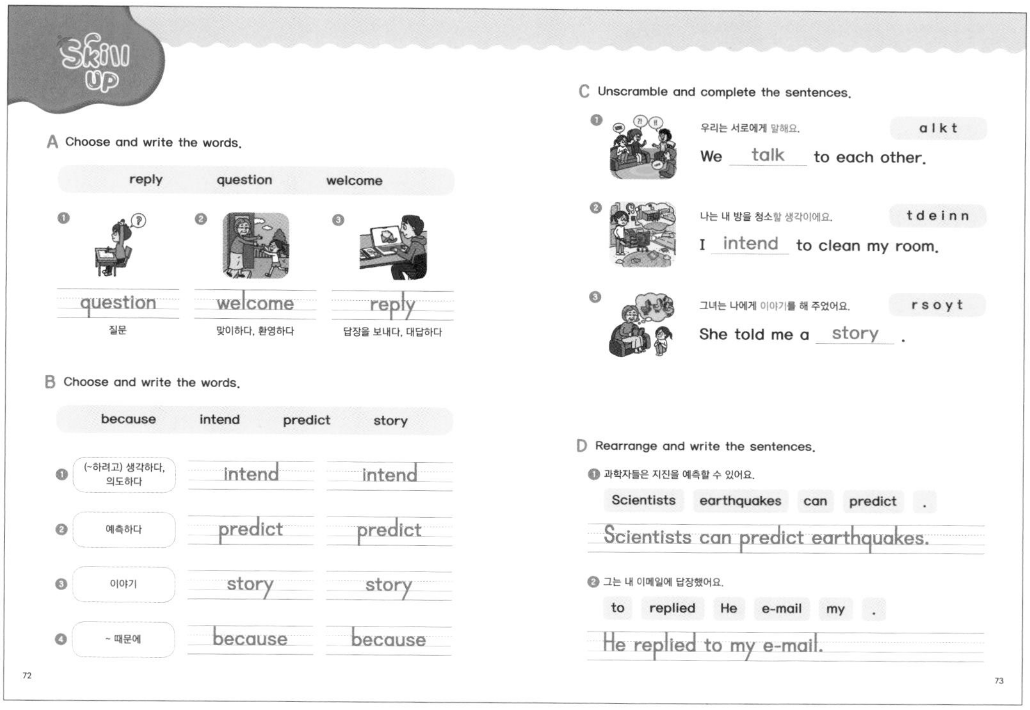
Skill up

A Choose and write the words.

reply question welcome

1 question 질문
2 welcome 맞이하다, 환영하다
3 reply 답장을 보내다, 대답하다

B Choose and write the words.

because intend predict story

1 (~하려고) 생각하다, 의도하다 intend intend
2 예측하다 predict predict
3 이야기 story story
4 ~ 때문에 because because

72

C Unscramble and complete the sentences.

1 우리는 서로에게 말해요. alkt
We talk to each other.

2 나는 내 방을 청소할 생각이에요. tdeinn
I intend to clean my room.

3 그녀는 나에게 이야기를 해 주었어요. rsoyt
She told me a story .

D Rearrange and write the sentences.

1 과학자들은 지진을 예측할 수 있어요.
Scientists earthquakes can predict .
Scientists can predict earthquakes.

2 그는 내 이메일에 답장했어요.
to replied He e-mail my .
He replied to my e-mail.

73

Day 06~10

P74

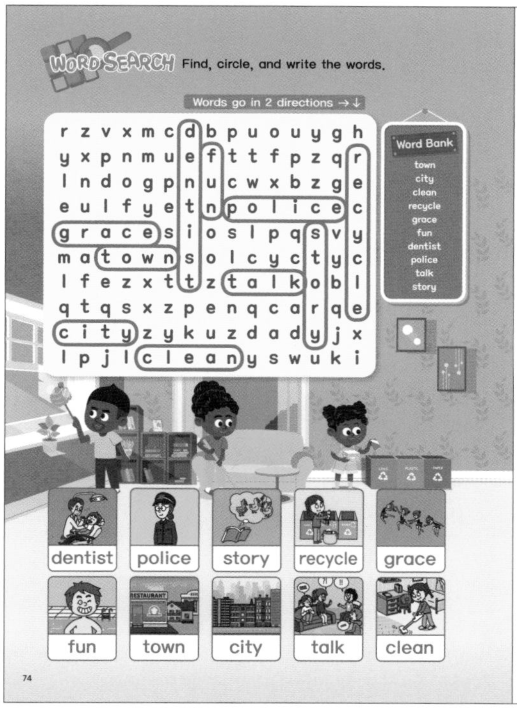
WORD SEARCH Find, circle, and write the words.

Words go in 2 directions → ↓

r z v x m c d b p u o u y g h
y x p n m u e f t t f p z q r
l n d o g p n u c w x b z g e
e u l f y e t n p o l i c e c
g r a c e s i o s l p q s v y
m a t o w n s o l c y c t y c
l f e z x t t z t a l k o b l
q t q s x z p e n q c a r q e
c i t y z y k u z d a d y j x
l p j l c l e a n y s w u k i

Word Bank: town, city, clean, recycle, grace, fun, dentist, police, talk, story

dentist police story recycle grace
fun town city talk clean

74

P76

Review TEST

맞힌 개수 : ☐ / 40

1 world	세계	21 장소, 곳	place
2 country	국가, 나라	22 빠른	rapid
3 city	도시	23 풍부한	abundant
4 town	소도시, 시내	24 먼, 동떨어진	distant
5 wash	씻다	25 주말	weekend
6 clean	청소하다	26 재활용하다	recycle
7 wait	기다리다	27 먼지	dust
8 stay	머무르다	28 세탁, 세탁물	laundry
9 famous	유명한	29 정직한	honest
10 great	훌륭한, 엄청난	30 우아함, 품위	grace
11 fun	재미있는	31 드문, 희귀한	rare
12 legend	전설적인 인물, 전설	32 잘생긴, 멋진	handsome
13 work	일하다, 일	33 꿈, 꿈꾸다	dream
14 dentist	치과의사	34 가치	value
15 police	경찰	35 체포하다	arrest
16 grow	재배하다, 자라다	36 투자하다	invest
17 because	~ 때문에	37 이야기	story
18 reply	답장을 보내다, 대답하다	38 질문	question
19 intend	(~하려고) 생각하다, 의도하다	39 예측하다	predict
20 welcome	맞이하다, 환영하다	40 말하다	talk

76

Day 11

P79

Pop Quiz ☑ 식탁 ☐ 식사 ☑ 메모 ☐ 붓

P82~83

Skill Up

A Find, circle, and write the words.

1. abrushfm — 붓, 솔질하다 — brush
2. qwbnotez — 메모, 쪽지 — note
3. nmealkgy — 식사, 끼니 — meal
4. tablemao — 식탁, 탁자 — table

B Cross out, unscramble, and write the words.

1. 카레 — cxuyrr — curry
2. (시간을) 보내다, (돈을) 쓰다 — despxn — spend
3. 검토하다, 복습하다 — exriewv — review
4. 식사, 끼니 — elaxm — meal

C Connect and fill in the blanks.

1. I need to review my homework.
나는 숙제를 검토해 야 해요.
2. I usually spend an hour at the gym.
나는 보통 체육관에서 한 시간을 보내요.
3. I often eat curry for dinner.
나는 저녁으로 카레 를 자주 먹어요.

D Choose and complete the sentences.

brush note strawberry

1. 나는 붓을 닦아요.
I clean my brush.
2. 케이크 위에 딸기가 있어요.
There is a strawberry on the cake.
3. 그녀는 책에 메모를 적었어요.
She wrote a note in her book.

Day 12

P85

Pop Quiz ☑ 고대의 ☐ 풍습 ☑ 이국적인 ☐ 바다

P88~89

Skill Up

A Choose and write the words.

weather exotic airport

1. airport — 공항
2. weather — 날씨
3. exotic — 외국의, 이국적인

B Choose and write the words.

sea custom ancient holiday

1. 휴일 — holiday — holiday
2. 고대의, 아주 오래된 — ancient — ancient
3. 풍습, 관습 — custom — custom
4. 바다 — sea — sea

C Connect and fill in the blanks.

1. We climbed to the top of the tower.
우리는 탑 의 꼭대기에 올라갔어요.
2. Thanksgiving Day is a holiday.
추수감사절은 휴일 이에요.
3. I visited an ancient mosque.
나는 고대의 모스크를 방문했어요.

D Rearrange and write the sentences.

1. 우리는 공항에 도착했어요.
We / at / arrived / the airport / .
We arrived at the airport.
2. 나는 외국 과일을 좋아해요.
love / exotic / I / fruits / .
I love exotic fruits.

Day 13

P91

Pop Quiz ☐ 이른 ☑ 늦은 ☑ 추천하다 ☐ 노력하다

P94~95

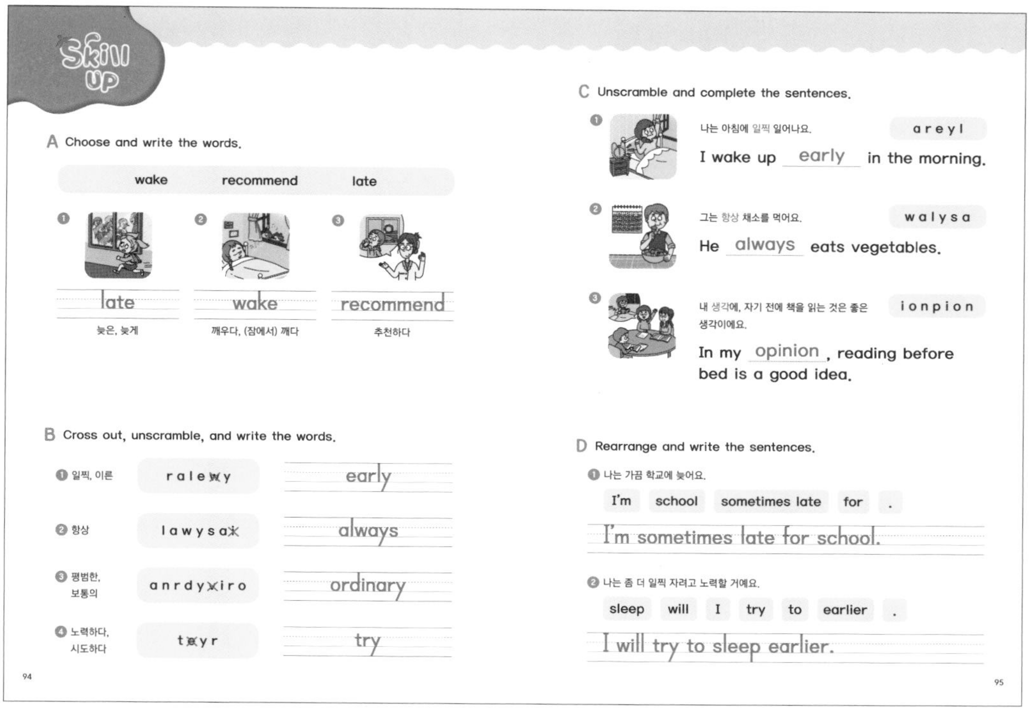

Skill up

A Choose and write the words.

wake recommend late

❶ late 늦은, 늦게
❷ wake 깨우다, (잠에서) 깨다
❸ recommend 추천하다

B Cross out, unscramble, and write the words.

❶ 일찍, 이른 ralewy — early
❷ 항상 lawysak — always
❸ 평범한, 보통의 anrdyxiro — ordinary
❹ 노력하다, 시도하다 texyr — try

94

C Unscramble and complete the sentences.

❶ 나는 아침에 일찍 일어나요. areyl
I wake up early in the morning.

❷ 그는 항상 채소를 먹어요. walysa
He always eats vegetables.

❸ 내 생각에, 자기 전에 책을 읽는 것은 좋은 생각이에요. ionpion
In my opinion, reading before bed is a good idea.

D Rearrange and write the sentences.

❶ 나는 가끔 학교에 늦어요.
I'm / school / sometimes late / for / .
I'm sometimes late for school.

❷ 나는 좀 더 일찍 자려고 노력할 거예요.
sleep / will / I / try / to / earlier / .
I will try to sleep earlier.

95

Day 14

P97

Pop Quiz ☑ 바쁜 ☐ 옳은 ☑ 고치다 ☐ 싸우다

P100~101

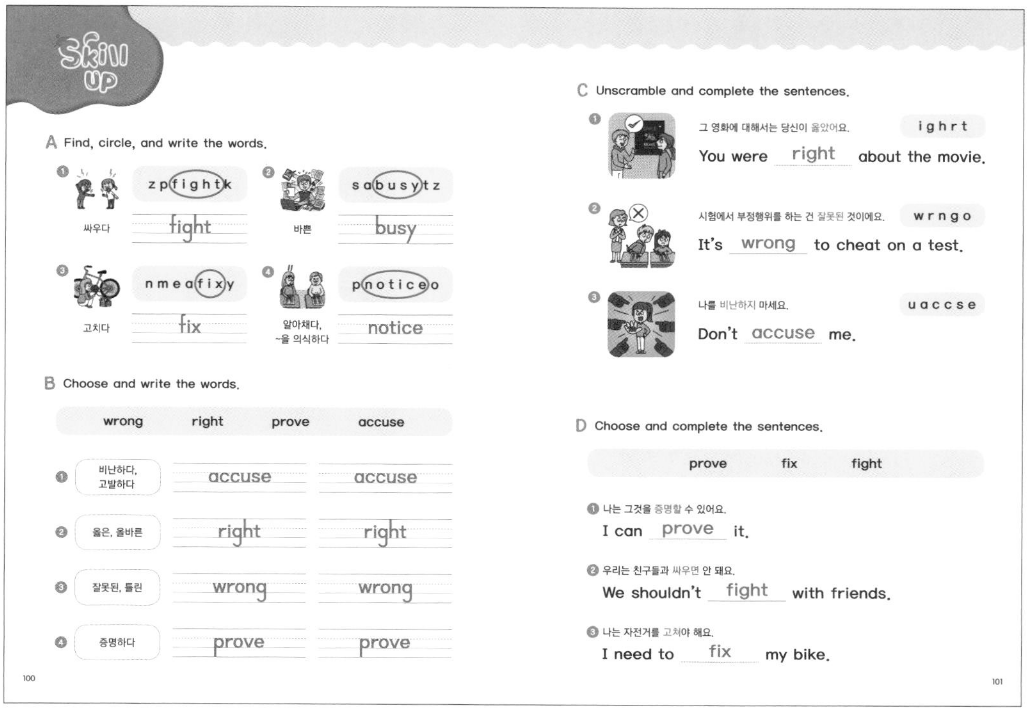

Skill up

A Find, circle, and write the words.

❶ 싸우다 zpfightk — fight
❷ 바쁜 sabusytz — busy
❸ 고치다 nmeafixy — fix
❹ 알아채다, ~을 의식하다 pnoticeo — notice

B Choose and write the words.

wrong right prove accuse

❶ 비난하다, 고발하다 accuse accuse
❷ 옳은, 올바른 right right
❸ 잘못된, 틀린 wrong wrong
❹ 증명하다 prove prove

100

C Unscramble and complete the sentences.

❶ 그 영화에 대해서는 당신이 옳았어요. ighrt
You were right about the movie.

❷ 시험에서 부정행위를 하는 건 잘못된 것이에요. wrngo
It's wrong to cheat on a test.

❸ 나를 비난하지 마세요. uaccse
Don't accuse me.

D Choose and complete the sentences.

prove fix fight

❶ 나는 그것을 증명할 수 있어요.
I can prove it.

❷ 우리는 친구들과 싸우면 안 돼요.
We shouldn't fight with friends.

❸ 나는 자전거를 고쳐야 해요.
I need to fix my bike.

101

Day 15

P103

Pop Quiz ☑ 대신에 ☐ 짧은 ☑ 달, 월 ☐ 해, 년

P106~107

Skill Up

A Choose and write the words.

date time past

① time 시간
② date 날짜
③ past 과거, 지나간

B Cross out, unscramble, and write the words.

① 짧은, 간단한 — r i ~~x~~ e f b — brief
② 하루, 날, 요일 — a y ~~k~~ d — day
③ 달, 월 — ~~x~~ o m h t n — month
④ 대신에 — s n ~~x~~ i e d t a — instead

C Unscramble and complete the sentences.

① 한 해가 거의 끝나가요. (e y r a) The year is almost over.
② 우리는 짧은 이야기를 나눴어요. (r i b f e) We had a brief chat.
③ 내 생일은 다음 달이에요. (o m h t n) My birthday is next month.

D Rearrange and write the sentences.

① 점심 먹을 시간이에요. (time / It's / for / lunch / .) It's time for lunch.
② 오늘 날짜는 며칠이에요? (the date / What's / today / ?) What's the date today?

106 107

Day 11~15

P108

108

P110

Review TEST 맞힌 개수 : ___ / 40

① brush	붓, 솔질하다	㉑ 딸기	strawberry
② review	검토하다, 복습하다	㉒ 메모, 쪽지	note
③ spend	(시간을) 보내다, (돈을) 쓰다	㉓ 식탁, 탁자	table
④ meal	식사, 끼니	㉔ 카레	curry
⑤ sea	바다	㉕ 공항	airport
⑥ tower	탑	㉖ 풍습, 관습	custom
⑦ weather	날씨	㉗ 외국의, 이국적인	exotic
⑧ ancient	고대의, 아주 오래된	㉘ 휴일	holiday
⑨ wake	깨우다, (잠에서) 깨다	㉙ 늦은, 늦게	late
⑩ early	일찍, 이른	㉚ 추천하다	recommend
⑪ try	노력하다, 시도하다	㉛ 평범한, 보통의	ordinary
⑫ always	항상	㉜ 생각, 의견	opinion
⑬ busy	바쁜	㉝ 고치다	fix
⑭ accuse	비난하다, 고발하다	㉞ 증명하다	prove
⑮ wrong	잘못된, 틀린	㉟ 옳은, 올바른	right
⑯ notice	알아채다, ~을 의식하다	㊱ 싸우다	fight
⑰ time	시간	㊲ 하루, 날, 요일	day
⑱ year	해, 년	㊳ 짧은, 간단한	brief
⑲ month	달, 월	㊴ 대신에	instead
⑳ date	날짜	㊵ 과거, 지나간	past

110

Day 16

P113

Pop Quiz ☑ 장소 ☐ 소풍 ☐ 점심 식사 ☑ 저녁 식사

P116~117

Skill Up

A Choose and write the words.

dinner breakfast lunch

❶  breakfast 아침 식사

❷  lunch 점심 식사

❸  dinner 저녁 식사

B Choose and write the words.

quick approve perfect picnic

❶ 소풍 picnic picnic

❷ 완벽한 perfect perfect

❸ 찬성하다 approve approve

❹ 빠른 quick quick

116

C Connect and fill in the blanks.

❶ 

❷ 

❸ 

This pizza is perfect!
이 피자는 완벽해 요!

I approve of her meal choices.
나는 그녀의 메뉴 선택에 찬성해요.

I packed the food for the picnic.
나는 소풍 을 위한 음식을 챙겼어요.

D Choose and complete the sentences.

spot dinner breakfast

❶ 우리 가족은 함께 저녁을 먹어요.
My family has dinner together.

❷ 나는 매일 아침을 먹어요.
I have breakfast every day.

❸ 이 식당은 아주 좋은 장소예요.
This restaurant is a great spot.

117

Day 17

P119

Pop Quiz ☐ 더러운 ☑ 자동의 ☑ 즐기다 ☐ 발명하다

P122~123

Skill Up

A Find, circle, and write the words.

❶  집 mzpf(home) home

❷  샤워를 하다 sf(shower) shower

❸  발명하다 m(invent)m invent

❹  기계 b(machine) machine

B Cross out, unscramble, and write the words.

❶ 자동의 uxatmtcioa automatic

❷ 더러운 rdyxit dirty

❸ 즐기다 eynojx enjoy

❹ 자주, 흔히 xftnoe often

122

C Unscramble and complete the sentences.

❶ 
나는 더러운 바닥을 닦았어요. idryt
I mopped the dirty floor.

❷ 
나는 세차하는 것을 즐겨요. eynoj
I enjoy washing my car.

❸ 
나의 식기세척기는 자동이에요. uaotmaict
My dishwasher is automatic.

D Choose and complete the sentences.

often machine home

❶ 나는 주말마다 집을 청소해요.
I clean my home every weekend.

❷ 나는 세탁기를 사용해요.
I use the washing machine.

❸ 나는 평일에 자주 빨래해요.
I often do the laundry on weekdays.

123

Day 18

P125

Pop Quiz ☑ 불 ☐ 기사 ☑ 구하다 ☐ 생각하다

P128~129

Skill Up

A Choose and write the words.

article shout save

① 
shout
소리치다

② 
save
구하다, 모으다

③ 

article
기사, 글

B Cross out, unscramble, and write the words.

① 불	i r f x e	fire
② 영웅	x e h o r	hero
③ 생각하다, 여기다	o n i s c e r d x	consider
④ 안전한	s x f e a	safe

C Connect and fill in the blanks.

① 
② 
③ 

That brave firefighter is a hero.
저 용감한 소방관은 영웅 이에요.

I need to find my key.
내 열쇠를 찾아 야 해요.

The fire quickly spread.
불 은 빠르게 번졌어요.

D Rearrange and write the sentences.

① 이 장소는 안전해요.
is This safe place .
This place is safe.

② 나는 산에서 큰 소리로 외쳐요.
I in shout loudly the mountains .
I shout loudly in the mountains.

Day 19

P131

Pop Quiz ☐ 오늘 ☑ 내일 ☑ 연습하다 ☐ 결혼하다

P134~135

Skill Up

A Choose and write the words.

marry practice crush

① 
practice
연습하다, 연습

② 
marry
결혼하다

③ 
crush
홀딱 반함, 강렬한 사랑

B Choose and write the words.

yesterday language today barrier

①	언어	language	language
②	장애물, 장벽	barrier	barrier
③	오늘	today	today
④	어제	yesterday	yesterday

C Unscramble and complete the sentences.

① 
몇몇 손님들에게 계단은 장애물이었어요. i r b a r r e
Stairs were a barrier for some guests.

② 
몇몇 손님들은 다른 언어를 말했어요. a l n g a u g e
Some guests spoke a different language .

③ 
오늘은 나의 결혼식 날이에요. d a o T y
Today is my wedding day.

D Choose and complete the sentences.

tomorrow marry practice

① 나와 결혼해 줄래요?
Will you marry me?

② 우리는 내일 신혼여행을 가요.
We are going on our honeymoon tomorrow .

③ 나는 춤을 연습해요.
I practice the dance.

Day 20

P137

Pop Quiz ☑ (시간이) 걸리다 ☐ 조사하다 ☑ 끝내다 ☐ 알리다

P140~141

Skill Up

A Choose and write the words.

hour minute report

❶ minute 분
❷ hour 시간
❸ report 보고서, 알리다

B Cross out, unscramble, and write the words.

❶ (시간이) 걸리다, 가지고 가다 — a~~x~~tek — take
❷ 끝내다 — ifnhs~~x~~i — finish
❸ 아직 — y~~x~~et — yet
❹ 절대 ~ 않다 — e~~x~~vner — never

C Connect and fill in the blanks.

❶ I finish my homework before dinner. 나는 저녁 식사 전에 숙제를 끝내요.
❷ I need to do some research. 내가 조사를 좀 해야겠어요.
❸ It takes ten minutes to walk to school. 학교까지 걸어서 10분이 걸려요.

D Rearrange and write the sentences.

❶ 걸어서 1분밖에 안 걸려요.
is It only a minute foot on .
It is only a minute on foot.

❷ 나는 이 닦는 것을 절대 잊지 않아요.
I to brush never forget teeth my .
I never forget to brush my teeth.

Day 16~20

P142

Word Puzzle Find and circle the pictures. Then write the words.

article fire hero home
machine marry report shower

P144

Review TEST 맞힌 개수 : /40

❶ breakfast	아침 식사	㉑ 빠른	quick
❷ lunch	점심 식사	㉒ 장소	spot
❸ dinner	저녁 식사	㉓ 찬성하다	approve
❹ picnic	소풍	㉔ 완벽한	perfect
❺ home	집	㉕ 자주, 흔히	often
❻ dirty	더러운	㉖ 자동의	automatic
❼ shower	샤워를 하다	㉗ 기계	machine
❽ enjoy	즐기다	㉘ 발명하다	invent
❾ find	찾다, 발견하다	㉙ 안전한	safe
❿ save	구하다, 모으다	㉚ 소리치다	shout
⓫ hero	영웅	㉛ 생각하다, 여기다	consider
⓬ fire	불	㉜ 기사, 글	article
⓭ yesterday	어제	㉝ 결혼하다	marry
⓮ today	오늘	㉞ 장애물, 장벽	barrier
⓯ tomorrow	내일	㉟ 언어	language
⓰ crush	홀딱 반함, 강렬한 사랑	㊱ 연습하다, 연습	practice
⓱ take	(시간이) 걸리다, 가지고 가다	㊲ 분	minute
⓲ never	절대 ~ 않다	㊳ 아직	yet
⓳ finish	끝내다	㊴ 보고서, 알리다	report
⓴ research	조사, 연구, 조사하다	㊵ 시간	hour

Day 21

P147

Pop Quiz ☑ 변하다 ☐ 따다 ☐ 단단한 ☑ 신선한

P150~151

Skill Up

A Find, circle, and write the words.

1 따다, 고르다 — g m (p i c k) m e — pick
2 과일 — s (f r u i t) o w z — fruit
3 차례, 돌다, 변하다 — a i (t u r n) t a — turn
4 단단한, 확고한 — v x h (f i r m) c — firm

B Choose and write the words.

vegetable fresh raw bunch

1 채소 — vegetable — vegetable
2 날것의, 익히지 않은 — raw — raw
3 다발, 묶음 — bunch — bunch
4 신선한 — fresh — fresh

150

C Unscramble and complete the sentences.

1 신선한 음식은 당신의 건강에 좋아요. e r F s h
Fresh food is good for your health.

2 나는 바나나 한 다발을 샀어요. u b n h c
I bought a bunch of bananas.

3 생채소를 먹는 것은 좋아요. w a r
Eating raw vegetables is good.

D Rearrange and write the sentences.

1 우리는 신선한 과일을 땄어요.
We fresh picked fruit .
We picked fresh fruit.

2 단단한 과일을 선택하세요.
sure Make fruits choose firm to .
Make sure to choose firm fruits.

151

Day 22

P153

Pop Quiz ☑ 서로 다르다 ☐ 가벼운 ☑ 들어 올리다 ☐ 무거운

P156~157

Skill Up

A Choose and write the words.

size force weight

1 size 크기
2 weight 무게
3 force 힘, 폭력

B Cross out, unscramble, and write the words.

1 무거운 — y x h e v a — heavy
2 가벼운, 밝은 — l x g h i t — light
3 들어 올리다 — l f t x i — lift
4 서로 다르다, 달라지다 — a v r y x — vary

156

C Connect and fill in the blanks.

1 — The rock is heavy. 바위는 무거워 요.
2 — This watermelon weighs 5 kg. 이 수박 의 무게는 5 kg이에요.
3 — The feather is light. 깃털은 가벼워 요.

D Rearrange and write the sentences.

1 나는 무거운 여행 가방을 들어 올려야 했어요.
lift I had to suitcase a heavy .
I had to lift a heavy suitcase.

2 자의 길이는 서로 다를 수 있어요.
of rulers The lengths can vary .
The lengths of rulers can vary.

157

Day 23

P159

Pop Quiz ☐ 어두운 ☑ 중요한 ☑ 다음의 ☐ 건너다

P162~163

Skill Up

A Choose and write the words.

dark pool change

❶  pool 수영장, 웅덩이

❷  dark 어두운

❸ 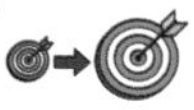 change 바꾸다, 변화

B Choose and write the words.

next important prepare traffic

❶ 차량들, 교통 traffic traffic

❷ 준비하다 prepare prepare

❸ 다음의, 그 다음에 next next

❹ 중요한 important important

C Unscramble and complete the sentences.

❶  길을 건너가자. orcss
Let's cross the road.

❷  교통체증 때문에 꼼짝 못 해요. raticff
I'm stuck in traffic.

❸  나는 회의를 준비할게요. reppaer
I will prepare for the meeting.

D Choose and complete the sentences.

important next change

❶ 다른 사람의 말을 듣는 것은 중요해요.
It is important to listen to others.

❷ 우리는 목표를 바꿔야 해요.
We need to change our goal.

❸ 우리의 회의는 다음 주 화요일이에요.
Our meeting is next Tuesday.

Day 24

P165

Pop Quiz ☑ 수업 ☐ 교과서 ☑ 방해하다 ☐ 집중하다

P168~169

Skill Up

A Find, circle, and write the words.

❶  olessonv — lesson 수업

❷  tlrufocus — focus 집중하다, 초점

❸  aquietad — quiet 조용한

❹  vrespect — respect 존중, 존경하다

B Choose and write the words.

begin interrupt textbook manner

❶ 태도, 방식, 예의 manner manner

❷ 방해하다, 중단시키다 interrupt interrupt

❸ 교과서 textbook textbook

❹ 시작하다 begin begin

C Connect and fill in the blanks.

❶ 

❷ 

❸ 

Please do not interrupt others.
다른 사람을 방해하지 말아 주세요.

Please talk in a respectful manner.
정중한 태도로 이야기해 주세요.

He borrows a textbook.
그는 교과서를 빌려요.

D Rearrange and write the sentences.

❶ 회의를 시작하자.
begin / Let's / the meeting / .
Let's begin the meeting.

❷ 도서관에서는 조용히 해 주세요.
Please / quiet / the library / be / in / .
Please be quiet in the library.

Day 25

P171

Pop Quiz ☑ 짓다 ☐ 들어올리다 ☑ 깃발 ☐ 생각

P174~175

Skill Up

A Choose and write the words.

build decorate approach

① build 짓다
② approach 다가오다
③ decorate 장식하다

B Choose and write the words.

triangle height flag idea

① 기, 깃발 flag flag
② 삼각형 triangle triangle
③ 생각 idea idea
④ 키, 높이 height height

C Connect and fill in the blanks.

I draw a triangle in my sketchbook.
나는 스케치북에 삼각형 을 그려요.

He climbs to the top of the mountain.
그는 산 꼭대기 에 올라요.

What a good idea!
정말 좋은 생각 이에요!

D Rearrange and write the sentences.

① 깃발이 바람에 흔들려요.
waves / The flag / the wind / in / .
The flag waves in the wind.

② 우리는 키를 쟀어요.
We / our / measured / heights / .
We measured our heights.

174 175

Day 20~25

P176

WORD PUZZLE Complete the word puzzle.

ACROSS
② The rock is ____. (heavy)
④ I bought a ____ of bananas. (bunch)
⑧ Let's meet at the ____. (pool)
⑨ What a good ____! (idea)
⑩ We need to show ____. (respect)

DOWN
① Let's ____ the meeting. (begin)
③ He climbs to the ____ of the mountain. (top)
⑤ Let's ____ the road. (cross)
⑥ I had to ____ a heavy suitcase. (lift)
⑦ Eating ____ vegetables is good. (raw)

176

P178

Review TEST 맞힌 개수 : /40

① raw	날것의, 익히지 않은	㉑ 신선한	fresh
② fruit	과일	㉒ 단단한, 확고한	firm
③ vegetable	채소	㉓ 다발, 묶음	bunch
④ turn	차례, 돌다, 변하다	㉔ 따다, 고르다	pick
⑤ weight	무게	㉕ 크기	size
⑥ heavy	무거운	㉖ 힘, 폭력	force
⑦ light	가벼운, 밝은	㉗ 수박	watermelon
⑧ vary	서로 다르다, 달라지다	㉘ 들어 올리다	lift
⑨ next	다음의, 그 다음에	㉙ 건너다	cross
⑩ important	중요한	㉚ 차량들, 교통	traffic
⑪ dark	어두운	㉛ 수영장, 웅덩이	pool
⑫ change	바꾸다, 변화	㉜ 준비하다	prepare
⑬ focus	집중하다, 초점	㉝ 시작하다	begin
⑭ lesson	수업	㉞ 태도, 방식, 예의	manner
⑮ interrupt	방해하다, 중단시키다	㉟ 조용한	quiet
⑯ textbook	교과서	㊱ 존중, 존경하다	respect
⑰ build	짓다	㊲ 생각	idea
⑱ flag	기, 깃발	㊳ 키, 높이	height
⑲ top	꼭대기, 맨 위	㊴ 장식하다	decorate
⑳ triangle	삼각형	㊵ 다가오다	approach

178

Word List

a

abundant	풍부한
accuse	비난하다, 고발하다
advantage	장점, 이점
again	다시, 한 번 더
aim	목표, 목표하다
airport	공항
always	항상
ancient	고대의, 아주 오래된
approach	다가오다
approve	찬성하다
arrest	체포하다
article	기사, 글
automatic	자동의

b

band	밴드, 그룹
barrier	장애물, 장벽
because	~ 때문에
beef	소고기
begin	시작하다
bill	계산서
both	둘 다(의)
breakfast	아침 식사
brief	짧은, 간단한
brush	붓, 솔질하다
build	짓다
bunch	다발, 묶음
busy	바쁜

c

change	바꾸다, 변화
city	도시
class	반, 수업
clean	청소하다
cold	감기
consider	생각하다, 여기다
cost	비용, 값
country	국가, 나라
cross	건너다
crush	홀딱 반함, 강렬한 사랑
curry	카레
custom	풍습, 관습

d

dark	어두운
date	날짜
day	하루, 날, 요일
decay	썩다, 부패하다
decorate	장식하다
delicate	연약한, 섬세한
dentist	치과 의사
dinner	저녁 식사
dirty	더러운
distant	먼, 동떨어진
dream	꿈, 꿈꾸다
dust	먼지

e

early	일찍, 이른
end	끝나다, 끝
enjoy	즐기다
example	예
exotic	외국의, 이국적인
expect	기대하다, 예상하다
express	표현하다, 나타내다

f

faint	어지러운, 희미한, 기절하다
famous	유명한
fever	열
fight	싸우다
find	찾다, 발견하다
fine	괜찮은, 좋은
finish	끝내다
fire	불
firm	단단한, 확고한
fix	고치다
flag	기, 깃발
focus	집중하다, 초점
force	힘, 폭력
fresh	신선한
fruit	과일
fun	재미있는

g

grace	우아함, 품위
great	훌륭한, 엄청난
grow	재배하다, 자라다
guide	안내하다, 이끌다

h

handsome	잘생긴, 멋진
headache	두통
health	건강
heavy	무거운
height	키, 높이
hero	영웅
holiday	휴일
home	집
homework	숙제
honest	정직한
hour	시간

i

idea	생각
important	중요한
instead	대신에
intend	(~하려고) 생각하다, 의도하다
interrupt	방해하다, 중단시키다
invent	발명하다
invest	투자하다

j

jog	조깅, 조깅하다

l

language	언어
late	늦은, 늦게
laundry	세탁, 세탁물
lawn	잔디
learn	배우다
legend	전설적인 인물, 전설
lesson	수업
letter	편지
lift	들어 올리다
light	가벼운, 밝은
lunch	점심 식사

m

machine	기계
manner	방식, 태도, 예의
marry	결혼하다
meal	식사, 끼니
minute	분
month	달, 월

n

never	절대 ~ 않다
next	다음의, 그다음에
note	메모, 쪽지
notice	알아채다, ~을 의식하다

o

often	자주, 흔히
opinion	의견, 생각
ordinary	보통의, 평범한

p

part	부분, 일부
past	과거, 지나간
perfect	완벽한
pick	따다, 고르다
picnic	소풍
place	장소, 곳
police	경찰
pool	웅덩이, 수영장
pork	돼지고기
practice	연습하다, 연습
predict	예측하다
prefer	~을 더 좋아하다
prepare	준비하다
proper	적절한, 올바른
prove	증명하다

q

question	질문
quick	빠른
quiet	조용한

r

rapid	빠른
rare	드문, 희귀한
raw	날것의, 익히지 않은
recommend	추천하다
recycle	재활용하다
reply	답장을 보내다, 대답하다
report	보고서, 알리다
research	조사, 연구, 조사하다
respect	존중, 존경하다
result	결과
review	검토하다, 복습하다
revive	회복하다, 활기를 되찾다
right	옳은, 올바른

s

safe	안전한
save	구하다, 모으다
sea	바다
shoulder	어깨
shout	소리치다
shower	샤워를 하다
size	크기
sorry	미안한, 안쓰러운
spend	(시간을) 보내다, (돈을) 쓰다
spot	장소
stay	머무르다
story	이야기
strawberry	딸기
stress	스트레스, 압박
struggle	힘겹게 하다, 허우적거리다

t

table	식탁, 탁자
take	(시간이) 걸리다, 가지고 가다
talk	말하다
test	시험
textbook	교과서
thank	감사하다, 고마워하다
thing	것, 물건
time	시간
today	오늘
tomorrow	내일
top	꼭대기, 맨 위
tower	탑
town	소도시, 시내
traffic	차량들, 교통
triangle	삼각형
try	노력하다, 시도하다
turn	차례, 돌다, 변하다

v

value	가치
vary	서로 다르다, 달라지다
vegetable	채소

w

wait	기다리다
wake	깨우다, (잠에서) 깨다
wash	씻다
watermelon	수박
weather	날씨
weekend	주말
weight	무게
welcome	맞이하다, 환영하다
work	일하다, 일
world	세계
wrong	잘못된, 틀린

y

year	해, 년
yesterday	어제
yet	아직